HANGED
in Error?

HANGED
in Error?

DONALD THOMAS

ROBERT HALE · LONDON

© *Donald Thomas 1994*
First published in Great Britain 1994

ISBN 0 7090 5357 6

Robert Hale Limited
Clerkenwell House
Clerkenwell Green
London EC1R 0HT

The right of Donald Thomas to be identified as
author of this work has been asserted by him
in accordance with the Copyright, Designs and
Patents Act 1988.

2   4   6   8   10   9   7   5   3   1

Photoset in North Wales by
Derek Doyle & Associates, Mold, Clwyd.
Printed in Great Britain by
St Edmundsbury Press Ltd, Bury St Edmunds, Suffolk.
Bound by WBC Ltd, Bridgend, Mid-Glamorgan.

Contents

1 Trial and Error

1

On 14 February 1948, Sir David Maxwell Fyfe MP, a future Home Secretary and Lord Chancellor, pitched into Sidney Silverman, R.T. Paget, and those members of the House of Commons who were arguing for the abolition of capital punishment. 'As a realist I do not believe that the chances of error in a murder case ... constitute a factor which we must consider.' His opponents disputed this but Sir David was unmoved. 'Of course a jury might go wrong, the Court of Criminal Appeal might go wrong, as might the House of Lords and the Home Secretary; they might all be stricken mad and go wrong. But that is not a possibility which anyone can consider likely. The honourable and learned member is moving in a realm of fantasy when he makes that suggestion.'

Forty-five years later, the Court of Criminal Appeal decided that it was Sir David Maxwell Fyfe himself who went wrong, as Home Secretary in 1953. He had denied a reprieve to Derek Bentley, who had been under arrest for twenty minutes when Christopher Craig fired the shot which killed PC Sidney Miles on a Croydon rooftop.

For all his faults, and they included a confusion in his mind as to how many policemen had been shot dead on that occasion and a mistaken belief that sixteen-year-old Craig had also been sentenced to death, Sir David merely shared the comfortable assurance of those in his position. The chance of a man or woman being hanged in error was so remote as to be irrelevant.

No one has been hanged for murder since 1964, but the policy of the Home Office is fundamentally the same in defining the role of the Home Secretary. 'He has a responsibility to consider representations that there has been a miscarriage of justice. It is, however, a basic principle of our system of justice that the decisions of the courts are free from interference. The Home Secretary would not normally consider it right, therefore, to exercise [his] power of reference unless there was some new evidence or consideration of substance which had not been before the courts and which appeared to cast doubt on the safety of the conviction.' It was this principle which hanged Derek Bentley, among others.

The briefest glance at the past might have withered such confidence as Sir David Maxwell Fyfe's. From three centuries of crime and punishment there had been executions of men and women who were certainly innocent. Others were very probably innocent. Some had committed the acts with which they were charged but might well not have committed murder. The most contentious group were those in whose cases the words 'hanged in error' constituted a question rather than a statement. A case at civil law is decided on the balance of probabilities. In a criminal case there must be proof beyond reasonable doubt. Too many of those accused of murder had gone to the gallows on a mere balance of probabilities or less.

Far in the past, nineteen-year-old Grace Tripp had been hanged in 1710 for a murder which was actually committed by her lover, who escaped prosecution by becoming a witness against her. In another case in 1721, William Shaw of Edinburgh was hanged in chains for the murder of his daughter Catherine. In the following year, when the family home was cleared out, her suicide note was discovered. The authorities acknowledged their mistake, though there was little they could do but take down from the gibbet-cage William Shaw's bones, which the birds had picked clean, and return them to the family for burial. In 1749 Richard Coleman was convicted and hanged for the murder of Sarah Green, during a brutal assault. He maintained his innocence. Two years later, James Welsh and Thomas Jones confessed that they had murdered young Sarah Green and that Richard Coleman had no part in the crime.

In a similar case in 1797, Martin Clench and James Mackley were hanged before Newgate Gaol for a murder to which three other men subsequently confessed. Shortly before Clench and Mackley were hanged, the gallows platform collapsed, taking the executioner, his assistant and the chaplain with it. The apparatus was hastily reassembled, but to some observers it seemed a supernatural warning that justice was not being done.

Even before the political and legal reforms of the nineteenth century, there were misgivings at the cavalier manner in which the law sped men and women to the gallows, for forgery and theft as well as murder. As far back as 1815 a greater disquiet over the shortcomings of the system was provoked by the case of twenty-one-year-old Elizabeth Fenning, a pretty servant-girl and cook who had been born in the West Indies.

Elizabeth Fenning's master, Robert Turner, was a partner with his father Orlebar Turner in a firm of law stationers in Chancery Lane. He and his wife lived a comfortable and prosperous life in Regency London, attended by their household servants. Elizabeth Fenning, whose prettiness made Mrs Turner a little uneasy, had been with the family for just six weeks. It was agreed that she was of previous good character. On 21 March 1815, she prepared some dumplings for dinner, which were eaten by the family and the servants alike, including Elizabeth Fenning herself. Within fifteen or twenty minutes, those who had eaten the dumplings were taken ill and began to vomit. Elizabeth Fenning herself was so ill that she said she would rather die than live.

Next day, Orlebar Turner, the senior partner, examined the pan in which the dumplings had been cooked. Fragments of the mixture still adhered to the pan and the liquid in its base showed a white sediment. John Marshall, an apothecary of Half Moon Street, examined the substance and pronounced it to be arsenic. There had certainly been arsenic in the house, where it was used for killing mice and rats.

Elizabeth Fenning was charged with the capital offence of attempted murder, as the only person who could have been responsible for the use of the substance. She was tried at the Old Bailey on 11 April. In her defence, several witnesses spoke of her excellent character. Mrs Turner, however, recalled a lack of respect shown by the girl and also reported that she had had to reprimand her for going into the male servants' room while not properly dressed. There was also said to be scientific evidence that the dumplings had been poisoned. The dough did not rise and the mixture turned the knives black.

The recorder summed up, pointing out to the jury that there could be no doubt of the dumplings being poisoned or that Elizabeth Fenning was the only person who had the opportunity of adding arsenic to the mixture. Moreover, he had been informed of four previous occasions when she had been guilty of murderous conduct, happily without killing anyone. All four stories were later disproved before an investigating committee but by then Elizabeth Fenning was dead. One story of her setting fire to a bed was at least true in a different context. It happened when she overturned a candle. At the time she was eighteen months old. On the present charge of attempted murder, she was convicted, sentenced to death, and hanged. Between conviction and execution she consistently denied her guilt. No notice was taken of experiments conducted on her behalf with arsenic, which showed that it did not prevent dough from rising nor did it blacken knives. As for the sediment found in the pan, it was not arsenic. Had it been, the entire family and servants would have been dead, not merely indisposed. In the quantity in which it was found, there would have been enough of the substance in the dumplings, had it been arsenic, to kill two hundred people.

So far as motive was concerned, Elizabeth Fenning had no apparent reason for such a crime. She was an attractive and eligible girl, who had repeatedly told her family and friends how happy she was during her six weeks with the Turner family. Whatever was wrong with the dumplings suggested that food poisoning rather than arsenic was the cause of vomiting.

There was no posthumous pardon for Elizabeth Fenning, no recognition that she had received anything but justice. Eleven years later, however, there was a case so scandalous that authority admitted its error. On 8 May 1826, the body of Benjamin Russell was found in Gleddish Wood at Brightling, Sussex. Once again, it was suggested that death was from arsenical poisoning. The dead man's wife, Hannah Russell, was proved to have bought arsenic, commonly used for killing rats and mice.

The victim's father, William Russell, alleged that he had

assisted another man, Daniel Leany, to carry the body to the wood from the house. It was assumed from this that Benjamin Russell had killed himself by taking poison and that his family tried to avoid the stigma of suicide by making it appear that he had collapsed on his way home. The post-mortem report referred to a white substance, arsenic, adhering to the mucous membrane of the stomach. The quantity was sufficient to have caused death in two to three hours. Arsenic in this quantity suggested murder. Daniel Leany and Hannah Russell were arrested by the constable. The constable testified that Leany said to him, 'Nobody can swear that either I or Hannah poisoned Ben Russell.' Turning to Hannah Russell, he added, 'If you don't say anything, nobody else can.'

The two suspects were tried at Lewes Assizes on 31 July 1826 for the murder of Benjamin Russell by administering a fatal dose of arsenic. Leany's defence was that he and Benjamin Russell had gone out that night to steal corn from Holloway's barn. As they returned with laden sacks through Gleddish Wood, Russell collapsed and died. But this defence was rejected by the jurors. Daniel Leany and Hannah Russell were convicted and sentenced to death. Five days later, Daniel Leany was hanged. Hannah Russell's execution was delayed by a technicality. She had been charged with murdering her husband, which was a specific crime of petit treason (the killing of a husband by a wife or a master by a servant), but there was now some doubt as to whether she had ever been married to Benjamin Russell. The marriage certificate was sought.

During this interval, Dr Gideon Mantell, who had attended the trial as a distinguished visitor, became very uneasy about the scientific testimony. The medical evidence referred to bruising of the neck and shoulders of the dead man, consistent with carrying heavy sacks. Moreover, sixty grains of arsenic was a huge dose but it would have killed the victim slowly, not in a few hours, and he would have been in very great pain. There was another case in the area where a woman had died and her body contained what was first said to be arsenic adhering to the stomach lining. On further examination, however, it proved there was no arsenic whatever in the body. But the most important medical evidence in the Russell case had not been referred to at the trial. Benjamin Russell suffered from heart disease. There could be no doubt, in Dr Mantell's view, that he had suffered a heart attack while carrying the sacks of stolen corn and had dropped down dead or dying.

The evidence, when presented to the Home Office, was so conclusive that Sir Robert Peel ordered the release of Hannah Russell. Daniel Leany had already been hanged, though now recognized as innocent of the murder. The only crime that he had committed was to steal corn from Holloway's barn.

Among other cases of the kind, Daniel Savage murdered his wife in County Waterford in 1815. Ten years later, Edmond Pine was arrested and charged as Daniel Savage with the murder. He did not look nor act like Daniel Savage and protested that, indeed, he was not the wanted man. Members of Daniel Savage's family said that Edmond Pine looked nothing like the murderer. But Pine was a simple soul who knew not how best to defend himself. He went to the gallows for what was almost certainly another man's crime, despite questions being asked in Parliament.

Other cases of the nineteenth century provoked the doubting response, 'Hanged in error?' rather than 'Hanged in error!' In 1887, the body of Miriam Angel was found in an East End lodging house in Batty Street. There was yellow staining round her mouth and frothing from it, which proved to be nitric acid. Under the girl's bed was a young man of twenty-two who lived in the same house, Israel Lipski. He was semi-conscious and had the same yellow staining round his mouth.

Israel Lipski was a Polish Jew who spoke little English. However, his story was that he had been set upon by two men on the first floor landing of the house. They demanded money and, not receiving any, attacked him. They forced a piece of wood into his mouth and poured the nitric acid down his throat, saying, 'If you don't give it to us, you will be as dead as the woman.' Thinking he was dead at last, they pushed his body under the bed in Miriam Angel's room.

Miriam Angel died of suffocation and had bruises to her face. The prosecution case was that Lipski came up the stairs, where there was a thin muslin curtain covering the internal window that looked into the girl's room. Perhaps there was a chink in the curtain or perhaps the morning light in the room was strong. Miriam Angel was lying half on her face and half on her side with her back to this window. Though the body was covered by bedclothes when found, the suggestion was that the girl had not been covered when Lipski saw her. Though he only saw her from the back, 'the legs, thighs and the whole of her genitals, and the lower part of her abdomen were exposed and not covered with her chemise. Her thighs were wide apart.' It was alleged that Lipski could not resist the temptation which Miriam Angel offered. He entered the room, presumably holding her from behind. When she resisted, he struck her, forced nitric acid down her throat and held her face in the pillow until she suffocated. Then he committed an act of necrophilia.

There was, however, no scientific evidence that intercourse had taken place. Though Lipski was identified as a man who had bought nitric acid, intruders in the lodging house might have laid hands on it as easily as he. Would he really have swallowed it himself? He was revived and taken to the London Hospital in Whitechapel Road, where he remained under police guard.

If Lipski had not had intercourse with the girl, what was the motive? The case was investigated by the improbably named team of Detective Inspector Final and Detective Sergeant Thick. The conduct of Lipski's trial by Mr Justice Stephen caused considerable controversy and led to the unusual spectacle of the judge defending himself in the press. As Martin L. Friedland wrote in 1984, 'Was Lipski properly convicted? I believe that he was not. The judge's charge was grossly unfair in stressing the "lust" theory and effectively took the case out of the hands of the jury. An appeal court today would, I think, quash the conviction.'

Against the claim of an unfair trial, however, was the fact that Lipski unexpectedly confessed to the crime the day before he was hanged. He claimed that he had intended to rob Miriam Angel but found no money. He also said that he had bought the nitric acid in order to commit suicide. The confession was made after constant visits by Rabbi Singer, who no doubt acted with the best intentions. But the story was, at the very least, odd. The confession was soon challenged in the *Pall Mall Gazette* by a reader who had known Lipski. On the very morning that Lipski bought the nitric acid, he was starting up a new business. Hardly the time when a man commits suicide. Moreover, the confession got the time of Miriam Angel's death wrong by two or three hours. According to Lipski, he slipped into the room to take what he could find before she woke up. Why, then, did he lock the door and make it harder for himself to get away again?

Such questions were unwelcome. Latent prejudice became overt anti-semitism, to the point at which the crowd outside the prison raised three cheers at the moment of the execution. By the time he confessed, having repeatedly and vehemently denied his guilt to that very moment, Lipski had lost all hope of reprieve. Was he persuaded that confession might in some way help his people or himself? Did he confess to shield someone else or in the hope of a last-minute pardon, if he told the authorities a story they wanted to hear? What could he lose? He went to his death leaving, at the least, a feeling that he had not had a fair trial and that the whole truth had never been told.

2

The twentieth century was to be equally troubled by cases of men and women whose executions left a mood of unease. Defendants were thought to have been hanged in error, either because they did not perform the acts for which they were put to death or, more rarely, because those acts did not amount to murder.

There was never a more controversial case of the latter kind than the trial of Edith Thompson in 1922. The circumstances were not disputed – it was their interpretation which was at issue. Edith Thompson was an attractive young woman with modern views and a lack of inhibitions. She worked as book-keeper to a milliner in Aldersgate and lived with her husband in Ilford. Percy Thompson was a thirty-year-old shipping clerk, in indifferent health. For about a year, Edith Thompson had been in love with Frederick Bywaters, a friend of both husband and wife. Bywaters, a laundry steward on a liner, was at sea much of the time but Edith Thompson kept in touch with him by letter.

On the night of 3 October 1922, the Thompsons were returning on foot from an evening at the theatre. Frederick Bywaters, home from his voyage, rushed from the darkness, stabbed Percy Thompson in the neck, and disappeared. Thompson was dead almost at once, though his wife ran for assistance, calling on passers-by to help. She knelt by the body of the fallen man, hysterical with shock and grief. Questioned by the police, she identified Bywaters as the man who had stabbed her husband.

It was futile for the two suspects to deny that they had been having an affair. Edith Thompson's letters found in Bywaters's possession seemed proof of it. But if the letters were to be believed, Edith Thompson had tried to poison her husband and put glass in his food while Bywaters was away. There was no evidence except her self-incriminating letters that she had done so and Percy Thompson did not seem like a man who was regularly being poisoned. Was the young woman simply making up stories to win or keep Bywaters as her lover?

The day before the murder she wrote another letter containing a passage that was to be used against her with fatal effect. This modern young woman who might have seemed every bit her own mistress fawned on Bywaters in her desire to be mastered by him. Worse still, it sounded as if she had incited him to commit murder. 'Darling – do something tomorrow night will you? Something to make you forget. I will be hurt, I know, but I want you to hurt me – I do really – the bargain seems so one-sided – so unfair – but how can I alter it?'

Examined dispassionately in a murder trial, such words made the bargain sound like complicity in the stabbing of Percy Thompson. Other evidence suggested that Edith Thompson behaved quite normally with the theatre party. She reacted with shock and hysteria when her husband was stabbed, refusing to accept that he could be dead. If guilty, she was either a superb actress or a hopeless conspirator. But the true evidence against her was the unsubstantiated claims in her letters. Even a phrase like 'do something tomorrow night' was ambiguous, to say the least. None the less, both Edith Thompson and her lover were convicted and hanged.

Without her letters, there was little evidence against Edith Thompson. Did those letters describe fact or fiction, truth or fantasy? A post-mortem examination showed no sign whatever that Percy Thompson had ever consumed poison and there were no scars such as might have been left by the

passage of fragments of glass. Edith Thompson protested her
innocence at every opportunity. Bywaters, facing the gallows
himself, made a statement swearing that the young woman
was 'innocent, absolutely innocent'. The tragic cry of 'I am
not guilty! Oh God, I am not guilty!' with which she greeted
the verdict of the jury, haunted those who heard and read it.
If Sir David Maxwell Fyfe truly believed that it was
impossible for a man or woman to be hanged in error, he
might profitably have studied this case.

The fate of Edith Thompson belongs to that group of
uncommon murder trials in which the actions of the accused
are not in dispute. The question is whether they amount to
responsibility for murder. Similar considerations were to
apply, in very different circumstances, to the death of
Margery Gardner at the hands of Neville Heath. Heath's
actions during their sado-masochistic relationship caused the
young woman's death. That he intended them to do so is, to
say the least, open to question. Edith Thompson's letters no
doubt incited Frederick Bywaters to an act of murder. Did the
foolish young woman intend this? Or did she merely seek to
posture before her lover in the pretentious self-dramatizing
role of a heroine who would kill for love? Did she intend to
spill blood with a knife – or merely ink with a pen?

3

When a man confesses to a murder for which another man
has been sentenced, the usual assumption is that the
confession is a bid for publicity or an attempt to save the
condemned man. To try a second man and, of course, find
that he could not have committed the crime after all, might
take six months or more. The law would not have permitted
the first man to be kept under sentence of death for so long.
He would be safely reprieved by the time that the second
man's trial ended in acquittal. Most men who have confessed
to the murders for which other men faced the gallows were
easily shown to be liars. In 1946, however, there occurred one
of the strangest cases of this kind. When it was over, for both
suspects, there was an uneasy feeling abroad that the wrong
man might have been executed.

On a post-war Sunday morning, 20 October 1946, the body

of a woman was found on a bomb site near the central shopping area of Deansgate in Manchester. Her name was Olive Balchin, a forty-year-old prostitute who had grown grey in her profession. She had been killed by blows to the head with a hammer. A hammer lay close by with some crepe paper in which it had evidently been wrapped. Norman Mercer, a local publican, identified the victim as a woman he had seen arguing with a man near the spot, at about midnight the night before. A shopkeeper remembered selling a man a hammer. The witnesses agreed that it was a man of medium height with dark hair. He was wearing a blue pin-stripe 'demob' suit, issued by the thousand to those leaving the army after the war. They did not agree very closely on his age, which was put between twenty-eight and thirty-five. According to the forensic evidence, however, the blows had severed certain arteries, causing blood to spurt from the body. The killer's clothing would probably have been heavily bloodstained.

Among those who had associated with Olive Balchin as a client, there was one obvious suspect. Walter Graham Rowland had a criminal record of violence. Twelve years earlier he had been sentenced to death for the murder of his own infant child. The sentence was commuted and in 1942, like many other prisoners, he was released for war service. On 27 October 1946, he was questioned about the murder of Olive Balchin, when CID officers found him sleeping in a transit dormitory.

Given his criminal record, Rowland seemed remarkably unconcerned by the inquiries. He had an alibi. He was home at New Mills that night, fifteen miles from Manchester. His hair was fair rather than dark, though it appeared darker from his use of brilliantine. His age was thirty-eight. If anything, he looked even older and more haggard, perhaps in consequence of the venereal disease for which he was receiving treatment. Rowland had been very upset when venereal disease was diagnosed. But if he had murdered Olive Balchin, it seems extraordinary that he now said to the police, 'It was a blow to find I had VD. I wanted to know where I got it. If I had been sure it was her, I would have strangled her. I did think it was her. It's hard to say it was her now. Had she VD? If she gave it to me, she deserved all she got.'

Rarely had a routine suspect offered the police so explicit a motive for a murder. As for identification, the shopkeeper who sold the hammer picked out Rowland as the purchaser, though Rowland did not fit the witness's previous description particularly well. Two other witnesses picked him out but less positively. One of these placed him in a café near Deansgate with Olive Balchin at 10.30 p.m. However, another witness in the café swore that the man was not Rowland. Other evidence, apparently confirmed by police records, showed that Rowland was in the Wellington public house at Stockport at 10.30, some six miles away.

Rowland's alibi was that he had gone home to his mother at New Mills, fifteen miles from Manchester, arriving at about 7.45 on Saturday evening. He had gone to collect his washing. He then caught a bus to Stockport. The bus was due in Stockport at 10.09 p.m., five minutes after the previous bus for Manchester left. If the bus arrived early in Stockport he could have caught the 10.04 bus back to Manchester, but there was no evidence of this. At Stockport, according to his alibi, he went for a drink at the Wellington public house. He named two police officers as having visited the pub while he was there and this was proved to be correct and was timed at 10.30 p.m. Rowland said that he then caught a bus to Ardwick in southeast Manchester, went for a fish and chip supper and found accommodation in Brunswick Street. His signature was in the register of the lodging house and the owner confirmed that Rowland was there at 11.40 p.m., when the house was locked up for the night. If this was true, could he have left the house which was then locked up, made his way from Ardwick to Cumberland Street, found Olive Balchin and started an argument with her, all within twenty minutes? The publican had seen the argument as he walked his dog at about midnight. It may be significant that he described the man as having 'a full round face', whereas Rowland appeared thin and sallow.

A further inconsistency was the forensic report, which suggested that the killer must have been heavily bloodstained from the severed arteries. Rowland had nothing but his blue pin-stripe suit. No blood was found upon it nor did any witness report seeing the suspect's clothes bloodstained. There was a spot of blood on one of his shoes which matched Olive Balchin's blood group, but that was all.

Against this defence, Rowland was a self-confessed thief, a proven liar in his first statements to the police, a man with a record of violence, and one who had a grudge against Olive Balchin, as he told his interrogators. He was the sort of man who might have committed the murder. The question was whether he was the man who, in reality, killed the woman. If he had done so, surely he would not have handed the police a motive so neatly packaged. Moreover, if the independent witnesses to his alibi were believed – and there was no apparent reason why they should not be – it was unlikely that he could have committed the crime.

Rowland was found guilty at his trial and was sentenced to death. He had quite a strong defence, but the jury preferred the Crown's version of events. Soon after the trial, on 22 January 1947, came one of the most dramatic developments in any English murder case, David John Ware, a prisoner at Walton Gaol, Liverpool, made a detailed and circumstantial confession. He described how he, not the man now under sentence of death, had murdered Olive Balchin. Ware had arrived in Manchester the night before. He had bought the hammer next day for use in a robbery. He picked up Olive Balchin and they went to a cinema near the Belle Vue Stadium. Afterwards, at about 10 p.m., they made their way to the ruins on the bomb site. Ware then realized that the woman had gone through his pockets and taken some money. He hit her with the hammer and she screamed. He hit her again to stop her screaming and continued until blood sprayed from her head. In a panic, he ran off, making his way by bus, on foot, and hitch-hiking, to Sheffield. There he gave himself up to the police for theft committed at Stoke-on-Trent.

The Court of Criminal Appeal dismissed Rowland's appeal based on evidence at his trial but indicated that the Home Secretary should inquire into Ware's confession. It was, to say the least, plausible and accurate in detail so far as the events other than the murder were concerned. The inquiry, led by J.C. Jolly, KC, assisted by Superintendent Tom Barratt of Scotland Yard, began work on 22 February, five days before Rowland was due to be hanged. Ware insisted that his story was true. Then, abruptly, he withdrew the confession. Rowland was hanged on 27 Februry 1947 and that seemed to be the end of the Olive Balchin case. Rowland, as might be expected, maintained until the end that he was innocent of the crime.

David Ware served his sentence and was released. In 1951, he was charged with a further crime committed in Bristol. This time it was attempted murder. He was found guilty but insane. He had told the police, 'I have killed a woman. I don't know what is the matter with me. I keep on having an urge to hit women on the head.' Had the urge moved him, five years earlier, to hit Olive Balchin on the head with a hammer?

4

Authority, let alone bureaucracy, is never quick to acknowledge its mistakes. Moreover, in cases like that of Walter Rowland it was not certain that a mistake had been made. He had a strong defence but it was not impossible that he had killed Olive Balchin. Even the confession of another man, later discovered to have a penchant for hitting women on the head with homicidal intent, did not make it utterly impossible that Rowland was the murderer. By 1951 there were strong grounds for questioning his guilt but perhaps no more. Whether he would have seemed guilty beyond all reasonable doubt after Ware's conviction for attempted murder was another matter.

However, such misgivings were soon overtaken by a case which garnered more publicity than any enjoyed by Walter Rowland or his predecessors. The reason for this was in part a matter of historical circumstance. It coincided with a growing belief in Parliament, if not in the country as a whole, that the system of capital punishment was an anachronism in the second half of the twentieth century. The question of whether men and women had been hanged in error was becoming submerged in a debate as to whether they should ever have been hanged at all. A single major miscarriage of justice would add incalculable weight to this humanitarian campaign.

On the afternoon of Sunday 30 November 1949, Timothy Evans, a twenty-five-year-old van-driver, walked into the police station at Merthyr Vale. He was slight in build and no less slight in formal intelligence. He asked for a private interview and confided to the duty constable that he had disposed of his wife Beryl and put her body down the drain. It had happened at his lodgings in London, 10 Rillington Place. The terraced house was in a shabby cul-de-sac just off St Marks Road, near Ladbroke Grove tube station. Evans explained that he had not killed his twenty-year-old wife but had obtained some 'stuff' in a bottle for her from a man at a transport café. It was a medicine for procuring an abortion. When he came home at night his wife, who had presumably taken the mixture, was lying dead. He had put her body down the drain.

While he was still held in South Wales, Evans made a second statement. He now alleged that Beryl Evans had died as a result of an abortion, performed upon her by the tenant of the ground floor flat at 10 Rillington Place, John Reginald Halliday Christie. When the young woman died, the two men had carried her body down to a temporarily vacant flat and Christie had promised to dispose of it by putting it down the drain. He also promised to make arrangements for the couple's one-year-old daughter Geraldine to be looked after. Evans had disposed of his wife's clothes and some of the furniture, while the hire-purchase dealer had collected the rest.

Scotland Yard descended on the terraced house in Rillington Place. It was apparent at once that Evans could not have put a body down the drain. There was no sign of a body and, in any case, the opening under the iron cover would almost certainly have been too small. But the premises were searched. On 2 December, in an outside wash-house, two packages were discovered. One contained the body of Beryl Evans and the other that of the baby daughter Geraldine. Both had been strangled.

Timothy Evans was brought back from Wales to London. Confronted with the new evidence, he admitted that he had killed both his wife and the baby. Beryl Evans had driven him frantic by the debts she incurred. He had strangled her first and the baby a few days later. He made a fourth statement, in which there was no mention of the abortion and no further attempt to incriminate Christie. On 3 December, Evans was charged with the murder of his wife. He replied, 'Yes, that's right.' When charged with the murder of the baby, he made no reply.

From then until his trial at the Central Criminal Court,

almost six weeks later, Evans mingled denial and admission. After the magistrates hearing, he told his mother, 'I never done it, Mum. Christie done it.' By the time that he reached the Old Bailey, 'Christie done it' was his defence. He had confessed to the police in part to protect Christie, out of misplaced loyalty, and in part because he feared the police would knock him about unless he told them what they wanted to hear. Evans was of low intelligence, though not obviously dim-witted to most of those who knew him. He was certainly not illiterate. Yet the more recent cases of those like Wayne Darvell, Stefan Kiszko and Stephen Miller have amply illustrated that suspects of less than normal intelligence are the most likely to tell the police what they believe the police wish to hear – if only as a way of ending the intolerable stress of questioning.

In the case of Timothy Evans, however, he went to the police before they came to him. Had he not done so and had Christie managed to bury the two bodies in the garden, might they not have escaped detection? It would have been difficult but not impossible for Evans, with the other man's assistance, to invent some story of going away with Beryl and Geraldine. Once in the hands of the police, however, he certainly showed the confusion and inconsistency of an ill-endowed intelligence.

The police knew something of Christie. He had been in the army in 1918 and had been gassed on the Western Front. He was now fifty-two years old and had served as a special constable during the 1939–45 war, being too old for military service. Surprisingly, in view of his acceptance by the police service, he had previously acquired a criminal record. In 1920 he had first served three months in prison for stealing postal orders while employed as a postman. He had also been prosecuted for assaulting the woman he was living with, at a time when he had temporarily deserted his wife. He had served several short terms of imprisonment as a result of his dishonesty, though he had not been in trouble with the law since 1933.

Despite his criminal record, the Crown presented Christie at Evans's trial as a man who had redeemed his past errors of conduct. He denied having had any part in the murders of Beryl and Geraldine Evans. After all, Evans himself had confessed to the crimes and had only in one statement implicated Christie as a lethally incompetent abortionist. But Beryl Evans had not died as the result of an abortion. Like her baby, she had been strangled. If Evans had nothing to do with the murder of his wife, why, for example, had he sold her wedding-ring for six shillings to a Merthyr Tydfil jeweller shortly after her death? Even if he was right in saying that Christie offered to procure an abortion for Beryl, why should Christie want to murder her, let alone strangle her daughter as well? It made no sense. Though Evans insisted at his trial that Christie was the killer, he could not answer the all-important questions which Christmas Humphreys for the Crown put to him in cross-examination. 'Can you suggest why he should have strangled your wife?' 'No,' said Evans, 'I can't.' 'Can you suggest why he should have strangled your daughter?' 'No.'

That was the end, so far as Timothy Evans was concerned. Whatever misgivings the jurors may have had over Christie's record were soothed by Christmas Humphreys's presentation of him as a man who served his country 'apparently with distinction' in two wars and had kept out of trouble for almost twenty years. Moreover, at a time when he was supposed to be carrying a body about the house, he was actually incapacitated by fibrositis. It took the jury two hours to find Evans guilty. The legal process passed him briskly on to the hangman. Pierrepoint executed him on 9 March 1950. Evans maintained to the last that, 'Christie done it.'

John Christie left Rillington Place three years after the case and the house was acquired by a West Indian immigrant. It was on 24 March 1953 that the tenant of the ground floor flat discovered an alcove in the kitchen that had been boarded and papered over. Inside were the bodies of three young women, naked or nearly so. The body of another woman, who proved to be Mrs Ethel Christie, was found soon afterwards under the floorboards of the house. The bodies of two more women were discovered buried in the back garden. Four of the victims had died since the execution of Timothy Evans.

Christie evaded capture for only a few days. He was arrested by a constable who found him staring at the river near Putney Bridge. The wanted man did not deny his crimes, indeed he embellished them. At his trial, his defence was one of insanity and his only evidence was psychiatric. If he was to be believed – and, in this matter, it seemed safe to do so – he was a homicidal maniac whose true pleasure came from strangling women during the act of sexual intercourse. This, rather than the much-discussed necrophilia, was his penchant. If true, it was at least not unprecedented. Havelock Ellis devoted a section of his *Studies in the Psychology of Sex* to the grisly phenomenon.

The two bodies in the garden dated from the war years. Constable Christie had strangled an Austrian girl, Ruth Fuerst, during intercourse in 1943. Muriel Eady was gassed to the point of unconsciousness in October 1944, then also strangled during intercourse.

Christie described how he had killed Beryl Evans, who at twenty years old was pregnant again and suicidal. He had caught her lying down with her face near the gas tap. The young woman begged him to help her kill herself and promised to let him do 'anything' by way of reward. Christie held the gas to her face until she became unconscious, then he strangled her. He claimed that because of his fibrositis, he was unable to have intercourse with her. But he did not admit murdering the baby, Geraldine.

Mrs Ethel Christie had died in December 1952. As Christie described it, the act sounded like the mercy killing of a woman who had become a nervous wreck and had just taken a fatal dose of phenol barbitone. He buried her under the floorboards. The other three women whose bodies were found in the kitchen alcove had been prostitutes whom Christie claimed that he had brought back to the house, gassed and strangled, between January and March 1953.

Christie was tried and hanged for the murder of his wife. If he also killed Beryl Evans then it had certainly not been in the way he described. The forensic evidence showed that she had not been gassed and that she had been struck a blow to the face not long before she died. Whatever the truth, Rillington Place had acquired a chilling resonance in the annals of English murder. The London County Council hastily changed the name of the cul-de-sac to Ruston Close. After the removal of so many bones, however, it was waggishly known in the neighbourhood as 'Filleted Place'.

It seemed inconceivable that a jury in 1950 would have found Timothy Evans guilty of murder if they had known that the only other man in the house had already strangled two women and buried them in the garden. Yet it also appeared undeniable that Evans knew of his wife's death, even if he had no part in it. It was by no means clear that he had no part. There was trouble between the couple and it had seemed unlikely that their marriage would last. If Evans knew that his wife had been murdered, to what extent was he involved in the crime?

Only Evans or Christie could have answered that question and both were dead before it was fully considered. In the week before Christie was hanged, a Home Office inquiry into the case was set up under the chairmanship of John Scott Henderson QC. Christie gave evidence at Pentonville prison but he was vague in his answers and added little to what was already known. The inquiry concluded that Evans had murdered both his wife and his daughter.

That was not quite the end of the matter. In 1966, there was a further report, after the entire case had been heard again before Mr Justice Brabin. The report concluded that it was 'more probable than not' that Evans had murdered his wife. Whether that would amount to guilt before a jury was another matter. On the other hand, the report concluded that Evans did not murder his daughter Geraldine. Perhaps he told the truth when he said that he believed Christie had arranged for the child to be looked after.

A man can only be tried for one murder at a time. Evans had been tried, convicted and hanged for the murder of the child. He had never been tried for the murder of his wife, though he had been charged with the crime. Now that he was cleared of the murder of Geraldine, he was therefore a man who had no conviction of murder against his name. He was given a posthumous pardon.

The Evans case was a *cause célèbre* as few of its predecessors had been. The good and the great campaigned against the way the law had treated him. Yet it was inescapable that he was involved in his wife's death. If he was innocent of the child's death, he was not necessarily innocent of murder. Elizabeth Fenning, Edmond Pine, Walter Rowland and their kind belonged to a quite different group. If they were hanged in error, it was because they had nothing at all to do with the crimes for which they were punished. Ironically, the same could not be said of the man who had received more attention than they ever did.

5

The chapters which follow show the doubts over conviction and sentence in individual cases. Those doubts come in varying forms and degrees.

In the matter of John Williams and the Eastbourne police-murder of 1912, there was evidence to show the defendant's guilt. Yet the sources from which some of that evidence came were so tainted, and the failure of any witness to recognize the accused was so complete, that the case against him seemed never to have been proved beyond reasonable doubt.

In the 1938 case of Robert Hoolhouse, there was no single conclusive link between the accused and the murder of his former employer's wife. Though he behaved rather suspiciously on hearing of her death, there was evidence to show that he could not have been the murderer. The case against him was so flimsy that there was an application for the charges to be dismissed during the course of the trial – and even an application for his release before the trial began. Why Hoolhouse went to the gallows seemed puzzling in 1938 and inexplicable the more the case was examined.

To suggest that a killer as notorious as Neville Heath might be in the least degree innocent of the lurid crimes with which he was charged is quite a different matter. That Neville Heath was responsible for the death of Margery Gardner in 1946 was not disputed. That he intended to kill her seems on later reflection most unlikely, and there was evidence not presented at his trial which might have shown this. Nor did anyone at the trial know that Heath's principal expert witness was giving evidence in a state of detached drug-induced euphoria.

Henry Jenkins of the 'Elephant and Castle Boys' went to the gallows in 1947. But was he convicted for what he was – a thug and petty criminal – rather than for what he did? He had a well-supported alibi. It might be thought, of course, that this was merely provided by a loyal family and by criminal associates. But of twenty-seven witnesses to the Antiquis shooting, including two who saw the suspect over a period of time, not one could identify Jenkins as being there.

The case of James Hanratty falls into yet another category.

He faced strong evidence against him for the A6 murder of Michael Gregsten and the maiming of Valerie Storie in 1961, and it might seem hard to show that he could be innocent. Yet there was so much that did not quite fit the account. There was the original suspect, Peter Alphon, who matched the profile of the A6 killer better than Hanratty in some respects. There was the unconvincing story of Hanratty from the London underworld, wandering on foot in rural Buckinghamshire, as if looking for a murder to commit. There was the independent witness who confirmed that Hanratty was in Rhyl at the time of the murder. Two sides in the case are represented by two utterly incompatible stories with some evidence to support each.

Finally, there is abundant evidence in the Lynette White murder case and others of the past twenty years that, had hanging been retained, a good many innocent men and women would have gone to judicial execution. Instead, they went to life imprisonment and were released when their names were cleared, in some cases ten or fifteen years later. These included a high proportion of those who were not only judged innocent but who, on later scientific evidence, could not possibly have committed the crimes for which they had been convicted.

At least these unfortunate people were not hanged. They lost many years of freedom but they regained their liberty at last. Yet this reassurance might seem too glib in the case of a man like Stefan Kiszko, who spent sixteen years in prison for the murder of a schoolgirl, Lesley Molseed, which on scientific evidence he could not possibly have committed. For sixteen years he was treated as a despised and hated child-killer in a vindictive prison population. What the ordeal of being under such threats and deprivations had done to him was unimaginable. He was released as an innocent man in 1992. In December 1993, his body was found. There were, according to the police, 'no suspicious circumstances.' It is true that the agents of his death were faceless and impersonal. But Stefan Kiszko had been destroyed by the figures of the injustice done him as surely as if he had died on the gallows.

2   The Case of the
Hooded Man (1912)

1

As the epilogue of lingering Edwardian summer moved to a close, it was hard to imagine any place less easily associated with gangs, firearms, and violent crime than the Sussex resort of Eastbourne. In the summer of 1912, the bands played favourite melodies of middle-class England, the iron spider-legs of the pier strode into the warm shallows of the Channel, and the Parade Police ensured that the wide and flowery esplanade was not infested by riff-raff. There was a sub-station just for this purpose, opposite the Grand Parade bandstand.

The etiquette of the promenade was under the benign surveillance of Parade Inspector Arthur Walls, forty-four years old, who had been appointed to the Eastbourne police force on the recommendation of the Earl of Chichester twenty-four years earlier, when he was a lad of twenty. He was known for his upright and gentlemanly bearing. The *Eastbourne Chronicle* assured its readers that he was 'well known to the great majority of annual visitors as well as local residents'. Arthur Walls was no crime-buster, just a nice man doing his job with courteous efficiency among parasols and spacious hotels, shrubberies and flower gardens, the bathing machines and promenades.

In the summer of 1912, most people believed that Arthur Walls's Eastbourne was just what it appeared to be. The theatre on the elegant pier offered its holidaymakers the undergraduate transvestite romp of *Charley's Aunt*. Family audiences rolled in their seats at the hoarse-voiced whiskery hero declaiming, 'I'm Charley's aunt – from Brazil – where the nuts come from.' For the more serious minded, the Devonshire Park Theatre staged a new production of Bernard Shaw's *Man and Superman*. P & A Campbell's paddle steamers *Brighton Queen* and *Glen Rosa*, with their white admiralty-top funnels, carried trippers on cruises to the grand Naval Review at Spithead or across the Channel to lunch in Boulogne – there and back for 40p.

But there was another Eastbourne, which the posters never showed and the wealthy seldom visited. Far from the expensive red brick villas and grand hotels towards Beachy Head, there were rows of little houses in streets beyond the railway station or down the shabbier length of Seaside, which was not truly beside the sea at all. It was an area of servants, artisans, shop-girls, and humbler lodging-houses.

Between the rich and poor were the new shops of Terminus Road, cinema entertainment provided by the Electric Theatre, the Eastern Cinema, the Cinema Palace and the quaintly titled Gallery of Illustration. Among the other good things of life, the latest open-top Studebaker could be driven away from Caffyns showrooms for £185.

Summer passed and, as the autumn evenings grew darker, the residents of Eastbourne had the town very much to themselves once more. Where the upper and lower promenades ran towards Beachy Head, a sweep of expensive houses rose above the main road on South Cliff, just beyond the palm court comforts of the Grand Hotel. Behind South Cliff, smaller but picturesque red-brick houses with white porches and verandas ran downhill again to Silverdale Road and the Meads. The house at 6 South Cliff Avenue was occupied by the Countess Flora Sztaray, daughter of a Hungarian father and English mother, who had long lived in England. Her title made her much in demand as a presenter of prizes at school fetes and skating galas. She had a talent for music and numbered among her friends both the violinist Fritz Kreisler and the pianist Jan Paderewski.

On the evening of 9 October, a little before 7.30, Countess Sztaray and her friend Mrs Fuller were going out to dinner at the Burlington Hotel. A coachman, David Potter, had been ordered to collect them in his brougham at 7.15. As he waited outside the house, a man came out whom he recognized as the Countess's hairdresser. Then, looking up, he saw the head and shoulders of another man on a ledge above the front door, outside the lighted window of the dressing-room. The Countess and Mrs Fuller came out, the Countess recognizing him and saying, 'Potter, you *are* a stranger. You haven't been here for a long time. Drive to the Burlington.'

Potter whipped up the horse and turned towards Silverdale Road. As he did so, he told the Countess that he had seen a man on the ledge above the front door. Countess Sztaray told him to turn back. He pulled up outside the house and saw her go in. She went upstairs to her writing-room and phoned Eastbourne central police station in Grove Road. 'Will you have a constable sent at once, as we have a man breaking into the bedroom window over the front door? A man is lying on the porch over the front door.'

Constable John Luck, who received the message, at once phoned Inspector Arthur Walls at the Parade police station. Two minutes later the Countess rang again and Luck said reassuringly, 'The inspector should be just about there now.' The Countess replied abruptly, 'They are shooting! They have killed my coachman!'

Luck turned to Inspector Pratt, sitting behind him, and gave him the message. Inspector Pratt got astride his saddle and set out from the central police station on his bicycle. One element of farce among all the melodrama was the revelation that the Eastbourne police had not a single motor vehicle. As a rule, there was only one inspector on duty at this hour. If he was overpowered or otherwise engaged, as one concerned citizen wrote to the press, the entire town would be at the mercy of banditti. By now the Countess was on the phone again. 'There is murder being done. Send someone on a bicycle.' Luck assured her that Inspector Pratt was even then pedalling with all his might through the lamplit residential roads of the Meads.

It was Arthur Walls on foot who had arrived at South Cliff Avenue first, walking down the hill from South Cliff itself. David Potter, the coachman, attracted his attention with a low whistle. Walls came across, went to the front door and spoke to the Countess, who was in the hall. Then the Inspector took a step back, shaded his eyes from the light and looked up at the ledge. It was possible to make out the man's head and shoulders.

'Here, old chap, come down!' said Walls. The unidentified

man moved to a sitting position and Walls stepped to one side a little among the shrubs, as if he might help him down. Without further preliminary there was a flash in the evening darkness and the crack of a firearm. Walls dropped to a stooping position and seemed to stagger towards the main road. The explosion frightened Potter's horse. Potter whipped him up and drove towards South Cliff. As he did so, he heard a second shot. At the end of South Cliff Avenue, he passed a man to whom he shouted, 'There is murder down the road! Give an eye and see if anyone comes this way.' He drove on to the cab-rank on the Parade, spread the news and went back to the scene with another cabman. At the inquest, it was suggested that he should have stayed to help Inspector Walls but Potter insisted that his horse was startled and that he could not keep the animal still.

Percy Moss, a cab proprietor, was at the end of South Cliff Avenue. Potter passed him shouting, 'Come to South Cliff Avenue at once. Police shot.' Percy Moss went the short distance and saw Inspector Walls lying on his back on the road. Moss spoke to him but, though Walls turned his head to him, the inspector could not answer. Another arrival, Helen Jones, was a parlourmaid from Silverdale Road on the inland side of the Grand Hotel. She found Walls gasping for breath, his clothes soaked with blood under the breast of his coat.

It was ten to eight. Someone ran to 3 South Cliff Avenue for George Flanagan, a surgeon, who had just sat down to dinner. Flanagan had heard the shots but thought they were a car backfiring. He came at once. It was clear that Walls was near death, unable to speak and groaning. Flanagan looked at the chest wound and thought at first that it might be a case of suicide. He asked if a revolver had been found. It had not, but Flanagan had no doubt of the cause of the wound. It was in the left side of the chest and, as the autopsy showed, the bullet had passed through the left lung and the heart before lodging in the right kidney. It had been fired downwards before the assailant jumped from the ledge. Within a couple of minutes of Flanagan's arrival, Arthur Walls was dead. The surgeon stood up. As he did so, he picked up a fallen trilby hat and handed it to a policeman.

Other police officers had now arrived, soon followed by Major Teale as Chief Constable and the horse-drawn police ambulance. The body was lifted on to the ambulance, covered with a rug from one of the carriages, and the inspector's cap laid on his breast by Major Teale. By 8.45 the news of the murder was public knowledge, displayed in the window of Arthur & Co of Terminus Road, a tobacconist's shop which also specialized in telegraphic news-reports.

2

The shadowy figure who had fired from the ledge above the Countess Sztaray's porch had jumped down, probably after firing his second shot, stooped to glance at the fallen policeman and disappeared. No one could identify him. Because he had been lying flat along the length of the ledge, his height was put at five feet six or seven inches. He was thought to be between thirty and thirty-five years old. That was all. It was also supposed that he had been attracted by rumours of the value of the Countess's jewellery.

There were few specific clues. A trio of two men and a woman had been reported loitering in South Cliff Avenue and the immediate neighbourhood on three days of the previous week. But it was an area which had become attractive to beggars and petty thieves. Seven days before the murder, Thomas Matthews had been gaoled for a week by Eastbourne magistrates for begging at South Cliff.

The only two items of evidence in police hands were the bullet which had killed Arthur Walls and the trilby hat, which had apparently fallen from the killer's head when he glanced down at his victim while running away. His need to get clear of the area took precedence over retrieving the trilby. It was a Kelvington trilby, size 7¼. Inside it was a paper label, 'No. 56. H062 8/6' and two letters which resembled a K written backwards and a P. This was enough for the police to trace it to Bournemouth, where it had been sold. Tress & Co of London had manufactured the soft felt hat and they had supplied it to Pearson Bros. of Bournemouth in April. Unfortunately for any hope of identification, Kelvington trilbies were sold in very large quantities and the number of Bournemouth's summer visitors rivalled Eastbourne's.

However, the link with Bournemouth confirmed suspicions that the man on the ledge might be a jewel thief rather than a casual burglar. The police revealed that there had been a spate of such crimes in Bournemouth and its surburbs, '... valuable jewellery being stolen, and the burglar or burglars getting clean away. It is now confidently believed that the Eastbourne assailant is connected with the Bournemouth robberies.'

At this point, Scotland Yard had assumed control of the investigation. Its senior officer on the case was Chief Inspector Elias Bower, described by a contemporary as 'a rough diamond, one of the old-time dicks'. He went to Eastbourne 'to have a tooth for a tooth, an eye for an eye for his brother policeman. He wasn't too particular how he got it.' Bower's reputation had been made in the Moat Farm Case of 1903, which had brought the womanizing Samuel Herbert Dougal to the gallows four years after his murder of Camille Holland.

Bower had every reason to think that South Cliff Avenue would prove less productive than Moat Farm. The threads of evidence were slender. There was no identification and, indeed, no suspect. But he had scarcely arrived in Eastbourne on 10 October when an opening presented itself. If it was true that Bower 'wasn't too particular' about how he got results, then the perfect partner had walked into Eastbourne police station.

Edgar Power called himself a medical student, though it was some time since he had studied medicine or anything else. One or two simple souls referred to him as 'Dr Power'. He was described as being about thirty, apparently well-educated, with pale, aquiline features and sleek black hair. Under cross-examination he was subtly evasive and repellent. His more recent occupations included a little blackmail. A few weeks before the murder of Inspector Walls, Power had been in the office of Horatio Bottomley, editor of *John Bull*, trying to market homosexual allegations against 'a wealthy and degenerate representative of an important English constituency'. He had been in company with John Williams. He now assured Bower that John Williams was the murderer of Arthur Walls. Williams had a revolver. Power was sure of that because he had seen Williams point it at his sister-in-law.

Bower checked the background of John Williams and

found that he matched the probable age and height of the man seen on the ledge above the Countess Sztaray's door. He had served in the army throughout the South African War of 1899–1901 and had been wounded in action. Since then he had acquired court-martial convictions and had served three prison sentences for burglary in England. He was said by the police to be able to climb like a cat and was suspected of being 'concerned in many daring jewel robberies at popular resorts around the South Coast'. Williams had no record of violent crime, however. His latest sentence of twelve months' imprisonment followed a London robbery at a fashionable apartment in Jermyn Street. Ironically, he was less of a rough diamond than Bower himself, being a genteel and well-spoken young man with a sense of style in his dress. He was known in West End hotels and among people of some standing. Inevitably, comparisons were made between John Williams and the currently popular creation of E.W. Hornung, Raffles, 'The Gentleman Cracksman'.

At Eastbourne police station, Elias Bower and Major Teale listened to their plausible informant with more hope than enthusiasm. Power had not told the Chief Inspector anything so far that would convict John Williams or anyone else of the murder. The day after the murder, Power had seen a card sent by the suspect to his brother, whose name was curiously similar and given in court as John William Williams. More curiously 'John Williams' was proved in any case to be an alias for George Mackay. Whatever the explanation, Edgar Power posed as a friend to both brothers. The card had an Eastbourne postmark. 'If you will save my life, come here at once. Come to 4, Tideswell Road, and ask for the name of Seymour. Bring some money with you. Urgent. Urgent.' Helpful Edgar Power had accompanied the worried brother on his journey.

They found John Williams lodging in one of the little houses of Tideswell Road with his mistress Florence Seymour, who was six months pregnant by him. As the conversation developed, his brother, who was well aware of his criminal past, had a chill suspicion that this was no ordinary financial scrape. There was also something very odd about John Williams's clothes. He seemed conspicuously over-dressed for the seaside in a silk hat and frock coat, as if he had no other hat. It proved later that he had a cap, but his outfit looked absurd in the little lodging house. His brother asked Williams outright whether he was involved in the Eastbourne murder.

'No I am not,' John Williams said. 'But I want to get away from this. I cannot do this without paying my board.' His brother gave him £2 for the bill and the two returned to London, leaving Power to follow later that day with Florence Seymour. Edgar Power had then excused himself for an hour and come straight to the investigating officers with his story. It was far the best lead that Bower had got. Having only just arrived in Eastbourne, he was soon on his way back to London, where Power was to report to him at Scotland Yard. Indeed, Power soon had another conversation to pass on. It had taken place when he had met John Williams that evening in the buffet of Westminster Bridge Tube Station. They discussed the murder and Power said derisively, 'You couldn't hit a haystack in a lobby.' John Williams said, 'Well, that was a good shot anyway.' 'What shot?' Power asked. 'That shot that all this disturbance is about.'

The exchange sounded damning but there was only Power's word that it ever took place. If Bower had wondered why his informant should have betrayed a friend so readily, he now began to see that the answer lay in Power's jealous passion for Florence Seymour. Perhaps that should have made the Chief Inspector a little more cautious.

Power became more helpful still. The next day, 11 October, two days after the murder, Bower decided to arrest John Williams. Edgar Power was to bait the trap. The false friend was to invite Williams for a drink at the buffet of Moorgate Metropolitan Railway Station and make sure that the suspect sat with his back to the door. As the two friends drank and chatted, Bower's officers burst in through the door behind their target, seized him and overpowered him. The Chief Inspector, standing in the middle of the station buffet, told Williams, 'I am a police officer and I am going to arrest you for murder.' Williams said nothing until the officers and their two detainees were in the police station.

Williams and Power were taken to Cannon Row police station, where Williams was charged with the murder of Arthur Walls. He said, 'I am perfectly innocent of this. I would not do such a thing.' Power had also been arrested to dispel any suspicions on the part of Williams or Florence

Seymour. Once Williams was charged, Power was quietly released.

John Williams refused to answer any further questions, but later he said to Bower, 'Do you think if I had done it I should have had the cheek to lie on that small piece of wood while the Countess was dressing?' 'It doesn't make much difference what I think,' Bower said firmly. 'Thinking won't alter it.'

But Williams persisted, 'Wouldn't it have been easier to watch the lights go down and the Countess go out, and then go in?' And that, at least, made sense. To lie in full view on the ledge with the lights on and the house occupied was surely not what a burglar of Williams's skill and experience would have done. It gained nothing and multiplied the danger of discovery. Bower said only, 'That's a matter of opinion.'

In itself, the arrest of Williams did little to forward the case. He insisted that he knew nothing of the murder. He had left Eastbourne because he was a known burglar and therefore likely to be a suspect during the investigation into Arthur Walls's death. Williams claimed that he thought he knew who had done the murder, though he could not prove it. Florence Seymour later recalled him pointing out to her two men and a woman in Seaside and explaining that they were known criminals. On hearing of the murder he said to her, 'I suppose it must be those two fellows I pointed out to you in Seaside Road.' Presently he added, 'The police know me and will accuse me of it if anyone that knows me comes down and sees me.' It was then that he sent the letter to his brother, asking for help in getting away from Eastbourne. Two men and a woman had certainly been seen loitering in South Cliff Avenue on three days in the week before the murder and Williams was not identified as either of the men.

It was the sort of defence which Bower might have expected, though it had logic on its side. As yet, the police investigation still relied too heavily on conjecture and circumstantial evidence. The trilby hat might belong to Williams, being the right size, or to any one of thousands of men. The bullet might have been fired by him but there was no gun, let alone proof, in the possession of the police. It was not a case that could be taken to a jury in its present form.

The partnership of Edgar Power and Elias Bower was

about to achieve its greatest success. According to Power, John Williams had owned a revolver. There was no sign of it now, though when they retrieved his luggage from the station cloakroom at Victoria they found a revolver holster, as well as a false moustache, in his trunk. Florence Seymour denied all knowledge of a gun. But the native cunning of Power rather than the forensic brilliance of the Chief Inspector saved the day.

Those who saw and heard Power in court were apt to use such terms as 'repellent' and 'abhorrent', not without reason. There were said to be murmurs of revulsion from the onlookers at the unctuous ease with which he betrayed one of his closest friends. Yet his masterstroke had fallen long before, on 15 October, just six days after the murder. Power went to Florence Seymour and explained that her lover was doomed unless they acted quickly. The former seamstress had no idea that 'Dr Power', as she trustingly called him, had been briefly detained by the police in order that Williams and she would still depend upon him. He assured her that the police were very close to the truth about where the revolver had been hidden. If they found it, they would have all the evidence necessary to send the father of her unborn child to the gallows.

Florence Seymour was in despair, her lover arrested for murder and she without friendship or financial support. 'Dr Power' promised to be a friend to her, for the sake of the man who meant so much to them both. He felt sure that she must know where Williams had hidden the gun and he was soon proved right. He promised that he would go at once with her to get it and dispose of it. The couple left London on the morning of 15 October by the Eastbourne train. When they arrived at the coast, Power first insisted that they should have lunch. It was after dark, at about 7 p.m., when Florence Seymour led him to the foreshore near the Parade bandstand. The revolver was buried there under the shingle. Power sent the girl down to the beach to get it. When she came back without it, he returned to the beach with her. This time, as Florence Seymour looked up from her search, a group of men were standing round them. Chief Inspector Bower and Sergeant Hayman were the principal figures. Power and the girl had been under surveillance since they left London, as Power well knew.

Florence Seymour was arrested. So was Edgar Power, for the second time in five days. The police took over the search, digging a trench across the shingle, an excavation which soon unearthed a dismantled and incomplete revolver. Though it was handled with great care, it proved to have been wiped clean of fingerprints. Before the two detainees were separated, Power had time to warn Florence Seymour that the police were going to charge her with murder, as an accessory. By this time the young woman was almost hysterical, or what the police surgeon called 'in a highly distressed and agitated condition'. In this state she was questioned until midnight and made a statement which did not accuse John Williams of murder outright. But her account increased suspicion against him to such an extent that it was likely to convict him of the killing, while it provided an escape for the girl herself. She described how they had walked along the promenade and sat on a seat near the South Cliff on the evening of the murder. John Williams had left her alone there for twenty minutes and had come back without his hat.

If she hesitated in her statement, Chief Inspector Bower need only have revealed another statement, made by Arthur Chase, a coachman of Silverdale Mews. Chase had driven along South Cliff in both directions at about 7.25 p.m. on 9 October. He saw Inspector Walls hurrying to answer the Countess Sztaray's call. And he saw a woman he believed he could identify as Florence Seymour standing close to the scene of the crime. She, who had at the worst stood and waited while her lover burgled a house, now found herself in danger of the gallows. She would not, of course, be hanged while she was pregnant. However, the pregnancy itself would almost certainly delay a trial until after the child was born. There would be no respite then. Florence Seymour was not a particularly bright or resourceful girl. Until the previous spring she had been a seamstress or a hospital nurse, according to varying accounts, before becoming John Williams's companion. On the night of 15 October, she faced her accusers alone and was plainly terrified.

Before the interrogation was over, Florence Seymour had collapsed on the floor and a doctor had been called. But Elias Bower had got the statement he wanted. The girl was then handed over to a police matron and remained in isolation from the world until the police court hearing at Eastbourne town hall five days later. She had one visitor. Edgar Power travelled down from London to show his concern and to assure her that she had done the right thing.

John Williams had already been brought from London on 12 October, first to Eastbourne and then to be lodged in Lewes prison for the hearing at Eastbourne magistrates court. Bower wanted his case established swiftly, before the young woman had second thoughts about her statement. Williams and his escorts arrived by train at Eastbourne station. A Napier car was parked opposite the coaches. The prisoner was brought out of the carriage, handcuffed to Bower and Sergeant Hayman, the upper half of his body draped by 'a dark blue fabric with white spots'. As excited passengers surrounded him, he was pulled to the car which set off with such enthusiasm that it knocked a small boy off his bicycle during the few hundred yards of the drive to the police station.

The prisoner was brought out again between two officers, the cloth still over his head and 'rapidly forced across the pavement to the entrance gates'. The purpose of the cloth was to prevent evidence of identification being prejudiced by allowing him to be seen in public. It was one of the first occasions when the police took such a precaution and it earned Williams the sinister sobriquet of 'The Hooded Man'. The precaution was unnecessary, however. No one ever identified John Williams as the man who had been lying on the ledge above the Countess Sztaray's front door.

On entering the magistrates court, Florence Seymour saw John Williams for the first time since his arrest. She looked, according to the *Eastbourne Gazette* reporter, 'delicate and terribly pale'. She stepped forward, held out her arms in her lover's direction and then collapsed in a 'semi-faint' and 'became hysterical'. The police-surgeon, Dr Adams, and a matron attended her. She was close to John Williams in the court and, as on other occasions, was plied with sips of water and whiffs of smelling salts to sustain her during her ordeal. As she came to give evidence, the smartly dressed prisoner said reassuringly to her, 'Cheer up, Flossie girl! It's all right!'

Examined by the prosecution, she repeated the story of sitting on a seat near South Cliff while John Williams was away for twenty minutes. But when Williams himself gently cross-examined her, she insisted that it was on Tuesday 8

October that all this had happened, the evening before the murder. On the night of the murder she had been with him at the Cinema Palace in Seaside. In any' case, she remembered he had been wearing a bowler, not a trilby, when they sat on the seat near South Cliff the day before. Though they had spent part of the summer at Bournemouth, he had never bought a trilby there, so far as she knew.

To his fury, Chief Inspector Elias Bower saw his principal witness recant. She did so in terms which suggested that Bower had taken advantage of her emotional and physical collapse at the time of her arrest, and that he had virtually written her statement for her. If Florence Seymour maintained her story of an alibi when the case came to trial, the Crown would have nothing but circumstantial evidence and surmise. Maintain it she did. Despite her statement made on the night of her arrest, she denied its implication to the first friendly face she saw, that of her lover as he cross-examined her. She had, of course, no legal advice or representation, either when making her statement or at the magistrates court. At this stage, even John Williams himself had no solicitor and was obliged to conduct his own case before the Eastbourne magistrates. By contrast, the Director of Public Prosecutions was represented by Treasury counsel before the magistrates, rather than by a solicitor. The outcome of the hearing was inevitable, however. John Williams was remanded in custody to face trial for murder at Lewes Assizes.

3

Elias Bower had no doubt improved his chances of convicting John Williams of murder, mainly in consequence of the assistance of Edgar Power. Whether he was any closer to establishing who had in reality shot dead Arthur Walls was another matter. The evidence in the case consisted of a chain of circumstances and allegations, none of them as strong as it should have been. Much would depend on whether a jury examined the strength of each inconclusive item or whether it could be persuaded that weak links sufficed to prove a case so long as there were enough of them. Much depended also on what they thought of Edgar

Power. As Williams's defence counsel was to put it, 'the character of Power, quite apart from the revolting nature of his betrayal, was such that no jury would believe his uncorroborated evidence.'

A Hastings solicitor, Harold Glenister, finally agreed to take John Williams's case. Sir Frederick Low K.C. was to lead for the Crown at the Assize Court. There was no money to brief a famous name for the defence. The solicitor at length found a young barrister who shared the name of the town where Glenister had his practice and who had never before appeared in a murder case. Thirty-two-year-old Patrick Hastings had fought in the South African War, like his client. While a law student at the Middle Temple he had read for the bar in the Inns of Court library by day while writing ill-paid journalism and theatre reviews by night. Having handed in his copy at 1 a.m., Hastings would begin his two-hour walk back to Putney, too poor to afford transport. Fortunately, he learned how to substitute brown paper for the inner lining of his shoes when they wore through.

Hastings had written unsuccessfully for the London stage in an attempt to finance himself while reading for his exams. Later in life he was to have greater success with a pair of plays. As it was, he passed bar finals without the necessary £100 to pay for his call. Though he managed to save £100 and fifteen shillings just in time, the wig and gown in which he was called had been obtained on credit. He made his way by sheer energy, ability, and an undeviating talent for plain advocacy. Hastings was to be Attorney-General in the Labour government of 1924. He was also to be one of the great names of the criminal bar, and he was to spend his entire working life at the bar with no desire whatever to become a judge. Apart from the chances of success or failure in his first murder defence, he saw the case with a dramatist's eye as having all the right ingredients: 'a gentleman burglar, a beautiful maiden, a false friend'.

The case against John Williams remained circumstantial, there being nothing else to connect him to the crime apart from Florence Seymour's original statement and the unsubstantiated report of what Power alleged he had heard the prisoner say. The revolver that had been found was in a state to support Williams's claim that he had bought it some time ago and that it had never worked. It had been wiped clean of fingerprints but, as Williams pointed out, this was not because he had used it to kill Arthur Walls but because he knew perfectly well that his fingerprints were on file at Scotland Yard. The trilby hat was one of many bought in Bournemouth and there was no proof that Williams owned one. His height and age were identical with those of hundreds of thousands of men. Oddly, he resembled Patrick Hastings to such an extent that when their photographs appeared in the newspapers at the time of the trial, Hastings wrote, 'it was impossible to tell which was which.' In any case, none of the witnesses who saw the man on the ledge above the Countess Sztaray's door could identify him as Williams.

Florence Seymour had told the magistrates that in her distressed state Bower had 'confused' her over dates when her statement of 15 October was taken. She could remember that she and Williams sat on the bench near South Cliff on the day they moved lodgings from Bolton Road to Tideswell Road. There was no doubt in her mind that it had been the same day. She had thought, under the stress of Bower's interrogation and the threat of a murder charge, that it had been Wednesday, 9 October, but she and other witnesses, including the landlady at Tideswell Road, proved beyond question that the move from Bolton Road to Tideswell Road was on Tuesday, 8 October. She and Williams had therefore sat on the seat near South Cliff the day before the murder, not on the day it was committed. Her statement was otherwise true, but Bower had browbeaten her into mistaking the day.

None of the witnesses of Arthur Walls's death could identify John Williams as the man who fired the shot, even though he was put on identity parades at Eastbourne police station. If Florence Seymour's evidence as she now gave it was accepted rather than her statement as originally taken, then the Crown had nothing much beyond two or three items of circumstantial evidence, plus the untrustworthy Edgar Power's uncorroborated assertion of what Williams had said to him in the buffet of Westminster Bridge Station. No jury who witnessed Power's performance was likely to believe him without corroboration. Apart from Power and the young woman, the prosecution depended upon little more than a trilby hat which might or might not have belonged to John Williams, and a revolver which was not in working order and which might or might not have fired the fatal shot. The jurors would scarcely hang a man on those two items. It was Florence Seymour's uncorrected statement that might still put the noose round his neck.

From the start, however, Patrick Hastings was uneasy over the case. Florence Seymour insisted that she had only made her original statement because Chief Inspector Bower had told her that 'unless she made a full confession she would be charged with murder, and that her only hope of escape was to incriminate her lover'. But she now added that she could prove which day she and her lover had sat on the seat near South Cliff. While they had been there on Tuesday, the day before the murder, she and Williams had heard a baby crying and they thought the sound came from 8 South Cliff Avenue.

A woman who passed by also heard the child crying. Florence Seymour and her lover had seen a man come to the door of the house and had heard him say, 'It is only a little temper.' But the woman was indignant on the child's behalf and said, 'I shall put it in the paper. I have a little girl myself and I feel for the child.' Florence Seymour was later able to identify the man, Mr Hole, who had spoken. While this would not prove that she and Williams were not there on Wednesday, it at least substantiated her story of being there on Tuesday and of having been confused by Bower over the dates. As for the Wednesday evening alibi, she and Williams were independently able to recall details of the films which they had seen at the Cinema Palace in Seaside. Though they could have seen them on another evening, it was apparently not on Tuesday nor any later day, since they then left Eastbourne. They could, of course, have seen them on Monday evening, but there was no proof of this. Like so much else in the case, this strand of evidence was tantalizingly inconclusive.

Even so, Patrick Hastings regarded the chances of an acquittal in the case with considerable doubt. Almost nothing in it seemed clear-cut, except the fact that John Williams was a known criminal. His real name was not even John Williams but George Mackay. Indeed, he was always 'George' to Florence Seymour. For that matter, her real name was not Seymour. She claimed to have been a dressmaker, but the newspapers insisted she had been a nurse. It made little difference except to suggest her capacity for telling untruthful stories. Mackay himself had adopted an alias because he was the son of a clergyman – his parents were still living in the north of Scotland and he had no wish to embarrass them by his criminal career. He had been well educated and had had a genteel upbringing. He dressed impeccably. For his trial, he wore a fawn coloured overcoat over a dark suit and white edged waistcoat. He also sported a black bow tie with white polka dots. A violin was among his luggage and he described himself on the charge sheet as a sculptor.

On hearing that Hastings had been briefed to defend him, Williams summoned him 'urgently' to Lewes prison. It was not clear why. Hastings demurred. 'The practice of such visits is most undesirable,' he wrote. He feared that his client might ask his assistance in concocting an ingenious defence, a practice he knew to exist. Worse still, the accused man might 'blurt out some statement or even confession' which would make Hastings's position impossible. Counsel cannot conduct a defence of the innocence of a prisoner who has told him that he is guilty. On this occasion, however, Hastings acceded to the accused man's request.

In profound gloom, the young barrister entered Lewes prison. He thought the experience was 'a horror'. The clang of the iron gates and the jangle of the gaoler's keys depressed his spirits but what was far worse was a visit to a man who, in all probability, might never come out alive. The horror, he recalled, became a nightmare. Yet it was Hastings who left the best sketch of John Williams – 'a remarkable person', as he called him.

> It was impossible to see Williams for the first time without some slight feeling of admiration. Whatever his crimes and faults, and they were no doubt many, he was at least possessed of the quality of unflinching courage. He showed not the faintest sign of fear or even anxiety. He said nothing about the facts of the case except to deny explicitly that he knew anything whatever about the murder. About the girl whose evidence against him was so deadly, he spoke with nothing but kindness; the only time he showed any feeling was when Power's name was mentioned, and

then he stated with a calmness that was almost startling, that if only he could get Power within reach for a couple of minutes there would be no necessity for anyone to defend him on a charge of murder.

Hastings left his client in no doubt of the danger facing him. The circumstantial evidence might be countered. The trilby hat, his departure from Eastbourne, even the revolver would scarcely convict him of murder. The great danger lay in Florence Seymour's statement to the police. However it had been obtained from her and however often she denied its accuracy, the details were public knowledge and would very likely have been read in the newspapers by members of the jury. It existed and could not be wished away. There was no hope of proving that Bower had obtained it by unfair or improper treatment of the young woman. Indeed, the Chief Inspector had become something of a local hero. The *Eastbourne Gazette* assured its readers that he was 'one of the most remarkable and efficient detectives of the century', a somewhat curious anticipation of a century that was not yet more than twelve years old.

Privately, Hastings thought Williams guilty of the murder. Privately and publicly he maintained that such guilt could not be shown by the circumstantial evidence. Yet John Williams's guilt was now put to the test by his counsel, when Hastings offered him a guilty man's way out of the peril in which he stood and Williams rejected it. Hastings asked Williams if he would like him 'to try for a verdict of manslaughter upon the possible ground that the shot had been fired without any intention to cause death'. A plea of manslaughter might well fail, but it seemed the most likely means of saving the prisoner's life. Williams brushed the suggestion aside almost with contempt, as Hastings recalled. 'I have been to prison before,' he said firmly, 'and although I am completely innocent, I would far rather be hanged than go to prison for another twelve months.'

In their lonely meeting within the walled silence of the prison cell, Williams's reply was one that an innocent man would surely have made. The temptation to a guilty man to save his neck by a plea of manslaughter would have been strong. Williams had only to admit being in South Cliff Avenue, firing a shot at random and in panic. But the

'Hooded Man' played for all or nothing. He was innocent, he had never been there. He would hang or go free.

Hastings left Lewes prison with a sense of awe at the composure and tenacity of his client, who might well be hanged before Christmas. But he never again consented to visit a defendant in his cell.

4

The trial of John Williams opened at Lewes Assizes on 12 December 1912. By this time there had still been no identification of him as the man who fired the shot. Everything depended upon whether the court would permit as evidence Florence Seymour's original and unmodified statement. There was very little new evidence beyond what had been produced at the magistrates' hearings, though the Crown called one expert witness of great future fame to give evidence as to whether the bullet found in Arthur Walls's body had been fired from the gun which Williams had hidden under the shingle near the Parade bandstand. The London gunsmith Robert Churchill, of Agar Street, The Strand, was to make forensic history sixteen years later. In the case of Browne and Kennedy, in 1928, his identification was so precise that the two men went to the gallows because Churchill could prove that the bullet which killed PC Gutteridge came from the revolver in their possession.

In 1912, as his biographer Macdonald Hastings remarks, 'Churchill could not prove that a particular bullet could only have been fired from one particular gun.... But as early as 1912 what he could say was that a specific bullet could only have been fired out of a specific make of gun.' In the case of John Williams's revolver, Churchill did not go quite that far. He had been able to get John Williams's revolver to work by supplying one or two new parts. Then he had to find a way of photographing the inside of the barrel. To do this, he filled the inside of the barrel with melted dentist's wax. The wax was then hardened by cold water on the outside of the barrel, after which the hardened cylinder of wax was eased out. The wax impression, of course, showed the inner surface of the barrel in reverse. But the impression was 'not sufficiently accurate for close measurement'. The wax itself was not sensitive enough 'to take the impression of significant pits and abrasions in the metal'.

However, the impression was photographed and the photographs were shown to the jury. What Churchill demonstrated was that Williams's revolver had the same number of grooves as had marked the murder bullet. That bullet showed grooves which were 'similar in width and in rifling angle as the test bullets', which he had fired from Williams's gun. They were similar but at this stage they could not be proved identical. Nor was there any means of showing that Williams's gun had been fired or whether he was telling the truth when he said it had never worked. After all, a revolver that did not work would still have its uses if it could bluff a householder. As for the coincidence of two similar revolvers being in Eastbourne, Williams's gun was of a common make and there were at least fifteen different makes of revolver with four grooves.

The danger to Patrick Hastings's case was that such expertise as the photographs of wax impressions was alluringly plausible to the members of the jury. Sir Frederick Low for the Crown, however, trod very carefully by saying that Arthur Walls had been killed by a bullet from a revolver which was no more than 'very much like' John Williams's. If that was the best that Low could do, he was in danger of being left with no case at all beyond the trilby hat.

The Crown's two most important witnesses, as at the magistrates' court, were Florence Seymour and Edgar Power. When Florence Seymour was called as the first major witness for the Crown, her reply to Sir Frederick Low might have been a torpedo amidships of the prosecution. She could say nothing. She could give no evidence. She knew nothing whatever about the murder. She insisted again that it was the night before the murder when she and her lover had sat on the seat near South Cliff. When the murder was committed they were at the Cinema Palace in Seaside. Sir Frederick Low at once asked the judge, Mr Justice Channell, for permission to treat her as a hostile witness, taking her line by line through her statement to the police. Patrick Hastings got to his feet. 'I wish to make a formal objection to the witness being treated as a hostile witness. There are reasons which speak for themselves why she should not be.'

Hastings's argument was simple and soundly based. A

defendant is to be tried upon the evidence presented before the jury, not on statements which have been made on other occasions and under obscure or disputed circumstances. The Crown was entitled to examine Florence Seymour upon her statement to the police in order to discredit her as a witness. In that case nothing she had said would be admissible as evidence. But the Crown was not entitled to examine her in order to discredit the defendant whose life was at stake.

Mr Justice Channell dismissed the objection at once, the first of his decisions unfavourable to the defence. Hastings knew that, short of a miracle, the case was lost. From then on, virtually every intervention from the bench was calculated to impede the defence and enhance the likelihood of a conviction.

Sir Frederick Low took Florence Seymour through her statement and perhaps in doing so got more than he bargained for. She was in tears much of the time as she fought for her lover's life. She now alleged that she had been to Scotland Yard immediately after Williams's arrest and before she had been tricked into going with Power to look for the revolver in the Eastbourne shingle. She had made a statement at Scotland Yard in which she said that it was the evening before the murder when she and Williams sat on the bench near South Cliff Avenue and when he went off for twenty minutes and came back bareheaded. On the following evening, at the time of the murder, they were at the Cinema Palace in Seaside, where there were six films concluding with *Dante* or *Dante's Inferno*. Before the last film, a man had sung 'Rose of My Heart'. They had gone to the cinema about 6.30 and come out at 8.30. Though the prosecution had denied at the magistrates hearing that such a film was shown, not only was it shown but before it on Wednesday evening Alec Davidson had sung 'Rose of My Heart'. Florence Seymour added that when Chief Inspector Bower saw the contents of her Scotland Yard statement, he refused to accept it. 'Perhaps he will produce the first statement I made at Scotland Yard.'

If Sir Frederick Low was knocked off balance by this, he soon regained his equilibrium. But Florence Seymour's statement remained an enigma. Had that statement been mislaid or had it never existed? Florence Seymour then described how she had been told after her arrest at

Eastbourne that unless she made a different statement to her Scotland Yard one, 'they would charge me and detain me' for the murder of the police inspector.

Her evidence was such that she could only defend herself by attacking the police, particularly Chief Inspector Bower whom the *Eastbourne Gazette* was praising as one of the most remarkable and efficient detectives of the century and who had proved that he never did anything more prejudicial to the defendant than 'ascertain the whole of the facts and present them in the clearest possible light'. But Florence Seymour insisted to Low that not only was her statement based on specific questions put by her interrogators, rather than a voluntary account of her own, but that Chief Inspector Bower had told her what to say by way of answers. An attack of this sort on the police in 1912 was a dangerous tactic, likely to harden the hostility of most trial judges to the witness and the defendant.

When Florence Seymour's ordeal was over, Edgar Power was called. He repeated his evidence against his former friend, including the unsubstantiated account of John Williams's self-incriminating comments. 'Never in my life have I met a more contemptible human being,' wrote Patrick Hastings afterwards. 'The betrayal of his friend was bad enough, but the story of his treatment of the girl, also according to him his dearest friend, must have revolted everyone who heard it.' As Power gave evidence, John Williams gripped the rail of the dock and several warders closed round him. It seemed that he might attempt to get over the rail and attack Power in the witness box.

Power's meanness of spirit was never more evident than in his smiling account when he told the court how he had tricked his friends. As Hastings cross-examined him, Power described how, after the betrayal, he had taken Florence Seymour to London on the 7.45 train from Eastbourne. He had also written to the girl to gain her confidence by promising to do his best to help her lover. In truth, he knew that he and Florence Seymour were under surveillance in order that they might lead Bower to Williams. Hastings asked if anyone else knew of this except Power himself. 'Presumably the police,' Power said with a humorous grin at the neatness of the reply. 'Don't smile at me, Mr Power,' said Hastings, and even in the transcript one senses a shudder at the smirking self-congratulation of the witness.

Repellent though he might seem, Power had made a friend in the Chief Inspector. After the case, Patrick Hastings heard that the police had rewarded their principal witness by smuggling him out of the country and had settled him elsewhere.

The case for the Crown had very little more to offer. For the defence, Hastings called John Williams himself. The prisoner's evidence was bound to begin badly because there was the matter of his previous criminal record to be disposed of. Hastings judged it best to be frank with the jury from the start, to admit that Williams was a burglar and thus to offer a reasonable explanation as to why he should have feared unjustified suspicion if he remained in Eastbourne. 'I must ask,' Hastings said, 'I think you have been a burglar.' 'Unfortunately so,' Williams replied.

Williams then began to explain the reasons for his conduct after the death of Arthur Walls. He had arrived in Eastbourne with Florence Seymour on 2 October, a week before the murder. Shortly afterwards they had seen a woman, about forty years old, with two men in Seaside. One of the men was 'Mike' or 'Freddy Mike', whom Williams described as a Continental thief. Williams raised his hat to him in acknowledgement. On the following Tuesday morning, the day before the murder, he had met Freddy Mike by appointment at the Cavendish Hotel on the seafront. They had a drink together and talked for about an hour. Freddy Mike gave him a coil of rope wrapped in brown paper and they arranged to meet again that evening.

So it was that he took Florence Seymour out for a walk to a seat near South Cliff Avenue. He remembered the child crying and, after his arrest, had been able to identify Mr Hole as the man who came to the door of the house where the child was. It was just before 7 p.m. and the only time he had ever walked along South Cliff Avenue. Leaving the girl on the seat, he then walked down the Parade to the Cavendish Hotel and kept his appointment with Freddy Mike, the other man and the woman. He was there for about quarter of an hour before returning to the seat near South Cliff Avenue. He had been wearing a cap that evening and returned without having put it on. It was folded in his breast pocket.

His evidence matched Florence Seymour's first statement

at Eastbourne of what had occurred on the evening of the murder (because Bower 'confused' and threatened her) and then what had taken place the evening before. Whatever immediate plans for robbery Williams and Freddy Mike might have concocted were evidently abandoned at their second meeting, and Williams told the girl to throw away the rope on the beach. It was found there soon afterwards by a workman.

On the night of the murder, Williams confirmed the girl's story. They had been to the Cinema Palace at about 6.30 and had come out two hours later. Walking along Terminus Road, they had seen the report of Arthur Walls's death in the tobacconist's window. Having involved himself with Freddy Mike and plans for jewel robberies in Eastbourne, Williams decided the best thing to do, on reading the report of the murder, was to get out of town. 'Being known to the police, it gave me rather a fright,' he explained. He sent the letter to his brother that evening and hid the gun under the shingle near the bandstand. The hammer of the revolver was missing, as indeed it was when the police found it. 'I bought it for two shillings from a Jewish fellow in the East End of London, and it was then in a useless condition and has been so ever since, as the hammer was missing.' He had bought it in a café in Commercial Road, Stepney.

Williams's story was exactly that of a man innocent of the murder. Unfortunately, it could only be explained by admitting to the jury that he was a professional burglar, indeed a thief since childhood, with an impressive record of convictions. Would the members of the jury put all prejudice in the matter from their minds and find a burglar innocent of murder?

Sir Frederick Low cross-examined Williams. Why had Williams first told the police that he had had the revolver during the South African War if, in truth, he had bought it less than a year before the murder? 'I am afraid I told a considerable number of fairy tales,' said Williams frankly. It was not a good start to the cross-examination. The lie had been unimportant to his defence but it now cast doubt on the rest of his evidence.

Low went through the more telling details of the case. Was it not a coincidence that a trilby hat, the size that Williams wore and which had been sold in Bournemouth, where he had been that summer, should have been found by the dead man? Was it not a coincidence that the victim was shot by a revolver 'very much like' Williams's? Was it not a coincidence that Williams, by his own admission, had walked along South Cliff Avenue the day before the murder? 'It is, rather,' Williams replied casually.

But that was not quite all. Williams's solicitor, Harold Glenister, was reported in the press as being 'engaged till the very last moment in searching for testimony in his client's favour'. He produced Sergeant William Diplock of the Eastbourne police. Sergeant Diplock had taken a statement from a man named Smith, a taxi driver. At 2 a.m. on the night of the murder, Smith had been called to the Grand Hotel, Eastbourne, by two men who told him to take them to the Queens Hotel, Hastings. The men were agitated and talked about the murder in some detail. One man got out in Victoria Drive, Eastbourne, before the cab went on to Hastings. Smith said that he was thoroughly frightened by the behaviour of his two passengers.

One of the men talked about a jewel robbery at a Brussels hotel while he was staying there. The other said, perhaps ironically, that the death of Inspector Walls was 'a terrible affair' and added that 'I always carry a pea-shooter.' Whether these two men were in any way connected with the murder, or whether they might be 'Freddy Mike' and his friend leaving Eastbourne in a hurry, was not established. Having made his statement on the day following the shooting, Mr Smith waited to be interviewed by Elias Bower and his officers. He never heard from them.

Sergeant Diplock told the court that he had taken a written statement from Smith and passed it to the inspector. It was now nowhere to be found. 'I heard of this statement for the first time last night,' Chief Inspector Bower insisted. It seemed unlikely. When Bower arrived in Eastbourne, the murderer was entirely unidentified. Smith had already made his statement. Would a statement involving two men who seemed such obvious suspects have been ignored? They talked of the murder, of jewel robberies, and one of them said he was carrying a gun. Surely Smith would have been one of the first witnesses to be interviewed, perhaps the only witness who might identify the killer. Before that happened, however, helpful Edgar Power had come to Eastbourne police station and told his story. It seemed that Chief Inspector Bower felt he need look no further. But how had Smith's statement been lost, since Bower insisted to the court that he had never seen it? Had he or another officer seen it and had it been suppressed? At the very least, the sole piece of evidence supporting Williams's story of Freddy Mike and the other man had gone missing under very curious circumstances.

The judge intervened to save the Crown's embarrassment. 'Mr Hastings, don't you think hundreds of people must have made statements to the police about the murder which probably amount to nothing?' But whether it amounted to nothing or not was precisely the question at issue. Hastings sat down, perhaps reluctant to antagonize the trial judge further. As his daughter, Patricia Hastings, wrote, 'One cannot help wondering whether he would have given way so easily twenty years later.'

A further statement which seemed to be missing was the first one that Florence Seymour claimed to have made at Scotland Yard on 11 October, in which she described how she and Williams had been near South Cliff Avenue on the day before the murder, not the day of the murder itself. It was the statement which Bower had refused to accept and which she said he made her contradict after her arrest on Eastbourne beach.

The only hope for Williams was that Florence Seymour would be believed about the visit to South Cliff on Tuesday and an alibi for Wednesday. It meant that the jury must believe that she tried unsuccessfully to tell her story at Scotland Yard on 11 October and was then made to make another statement on 15 October after her arrest. She had been hysterical and in fear of her life during that interrogation. She had withdrawn that version of events at the first opportunity. Moreover, the defence argued, a statement made to Bower was not evidence before the jury. It was what Florence Seymour said before the jurors that was evidence in law.

Mr Justice Channell ignored this and summed up for a conviction by telling the jury that if they accepted as evidence the statement made by Florence Seymour to Bower at Eastbourne, which he had ruled that they could do, they should find Williams guilty of murder. After that, Hastings had no doubt as to the outcome of the case. The jury went out and came back only fifteen minutes later with a verdict of guilty. Williams repeated, 'I should like to say once again that I am innocent of the charge.' He was then sentenced to death.

Hastings lodged an appeal on Williams's behalf on the grounds that a statement made elsewhere is not evidence before a jury. The judge had misdirected the jury on this. Before the Appeal Court hearing, the child of Florence Seymour and John Williams was born. Because of her 'notoriety', no hospital would take her in. It was left to Hastings and his wife to make arrangements for her confinement.

The appeal was heard by the Lord Chief Justice, Lord Alverstone. Hastings was 'not greatly impressed by his legal acumen. From the outset of the hearing it was apparent that he was satisfied of the prisoner's guilt, and no legal argument seemed to make the least impression upon him. Indeed in his judgment he never referred to it.'

The appeal was dismissed. But now there were misgivings over the case. Without Florence Seymour's statement, the case against Williams was circumstantial and weak. Once again, in a sworn statement to the Home Office, she insisted that the statement had been extracted from her by Bower 'by the use of threats'. A good many people believed her.

The national conscience was stirred as much by the conduct of the case and the investigation as by the evidence. Petitions demanding a reprieve for John Williams attracted a substantial number of signatures. Questions were put in Parliament by members of all three political parties with the aim of persuading the Home Secretary in the Liberal government, Reginald McKenna, to grant a reprieve. Robert Munro, the Liberal member for Wick Burghs, in whose constituency Williams's parents lived, moved the adjournment of the House on the issue. The Home Secretary was unmoved, insisting that he would only intervene 'if there were any subsequent evidence brought forward which would justify reconsideration of the case'.

The doubt haunting many minds was not simply whether Williams had killed Arthur Walls but whether it had been proved that he did. The circumstances of Florence Seymour's confession were such that there remained two sharply divided alternatives. Either Elias Bower was the detective of the century after all, or he was as cynical and unscrupulous as some opinions suggested. In that event, he had no hesitation in terrifying an already hysterical young woman with threats of the gallows until she was prepared to say whatever he put into her mouth.

John Williams was not to be saved. On the day before his execution, he was visited by Florence Seymour, who brought the baby with her. Though they were separated by a grille during the interview, he asked to be allowed to hold the baby. The warder took the child from its mother and handed it to him. Williams kissed it and pressed a small piece of prison bread into its hand. 'Now,' he said, 'nobody can ever say that your father has not given you anything.' He died on the following morning with calmness and quiet courage. Despite the usual admonition to clear his conscience before he was hanged, he maintained his innocence.

3 A Likely Suspect (1938)

1

19 January 1938 was a cold dry morning with a sharp east wind blowing across farmland just north of the industrial estuary of the River Tees. High Grange Farm lay five hundred yards up a cinder track, across ploughland from the A19, a mile or so north of Billingham. Several miles away, beyond the estuary and the salt marshes of the Tees, lay the blast-furnaces and rolling-mills, the coal wharves and 'the little brown streets' of workers' terraces in Middlesbrough. The 'infant Hercules', as W.E. Gladstone called the city, had grown from a population of just over a hundred in the decade of Victoria's accession to almost one hundred thousand in the year of her death. In the winter of 1938 the bleak ploughland and the industrial depression of the area combined to suggest a landscape that might have graced a novel by Emile Zola.

On that cold January morning, Henry Dobson left his farmhouse to walk to the nearby village of Wolviston. By now in his seventies, Mr Dobson and his wife Margaret, sixty-seven, had farmed at High Grange for many years. He had been up early that morning as usual. Bertram Smith and a team of threshers had arrived, having brought their machine to the farm on the previous afternoon.

Henry Dobson was on his way to Wolviston, about a mile distant, because by now he was concerned over his wife. She had set out the previous afternoon to go shopping in the village. Mr Dobson put the time at about 4.30, just as it was beginning to get dark, though he was a little vague about it. Mrs Dobson had said that if she was not back by 6 p.m., she would have gone by bus into West Hartlepool, five or six miles to the northeast. Mr Dobson assumed that she had done so. He went down the cinder track to meet the last three buses of the night, which stopped nearby on the main road, but his wife was not on any of them. He then thought that she might have received a telephone message or telegram from their daughter, presumably while she was in Wolviston, and that she had then gone to Newcastle, where the daughter lived.

By next morning, when his wife had still not been in touch with him, Mr Dobson decided to go to the village and make enquiries. Leaving the threshers at their work, he pulled on his rubber boots and set off across the fields, a shorter route than the cinder track. As he did so, he looked back at the cinder track and saw something lying under its grass verge, just where the ploughed field began. Walking back, he found the body of his wife. There was blood on her face, her clothes were disordered, her knees bent up and feet apart. The old lady had been raped as well as murdered.

Henry Dobson touched nothing. He walked on to Wolviston and found Police Constable John Chapman. Chapman in turn alerted the local doctor, James Craven. The three of them drove back in Dr Craven's car to High Grange Farm. It was evident to Craven that Mrs Dobson had been dead since the previous day. She had almost certainly been attacked and murdered about ten minutes after leaving home, some fifty yards short of the main road. There was ample evidence of the brutal assault which had preceded her death and she was described as being 'matted' with the semen of her attacker. The cause of death was two stab wounds to the neck and chest, either of which would have proved fatal.

Superintendent George Kirkup, leading the murder investigation, reached High Grange Farm at about noon. There was no sign of a weapon at the scene of the murder nor of any other evidence that might identify the killer, except perhaps footprints in the soil. Because the weather was dry and cold, the soil had not taken prints easily. Indeed, on the raised ridges of the ploughland it had not taken them at all. However, while the body was moved to the Isolation Hospital at West Hartlepool, plaster casts of the prints were taken by Detective Sergeant Edward Foster. Most of the prints had been made by the rubber boots of Henry Dobson as he walked round the body. In addition, there was a heel print which intersected with one of his and might well have been made by the murderer.

Mrs Dobson's handbag and her leather shopping-bag with a spare pair of shoes in it were found with her body. Her woollen gloves were still on her hands. There were other marks made by her shoes which suggested that after she had fallen or been knocked down, she had tried to get up by flexing her knees and pushing herself backwards with her heels. Her dentures were found close to her body, perhaps indicating that she had fallen heavily or been knocked down with considerable force. She had been wearing a small wig or toupee which was also found.

Two days later, on the afternoon of 21 January, Dr Henry Cookson, pathologist at Sunderland Royal Infirmary, carried out a post-mortem examination of the body at West Hartlepool. The two fatal wounds had been made by a blade penetrating to an inch and a half and being about half an inch wide. The wound to the neck had penetrated the inner jugular vein. However, as Dr Cookson pointed out, the blood from that wound had gone into the deep tissues of the neck and the chest cavity rather than spurting from the body. He thought that the victim could not have lived for more than five or six minutes after the infliction of such wounds. As for the sexual assault, he confirmed that Mrs Dobson had been raped, to judge by the violence of sexual intercourse and, indeed, Dr Cookson suggested that previous removal of her womb and ovaries would have made her own desire for intercourse unlikely.

There was food on which the process of digestion was not far advanced, since none of it had yet begun to leave the stomach. Unless there was some abnormality of the digestive system to slow down the process, which was apparently not the case with Mrs Dobson, this indicated that she had eaten about half an hour before her death.

2

As matters stood, Henry Dobson was the last person to have seen his wife alive, though there was never any suggestion that he was responsible for her death. On the previous afternoon, 18 January, there had been two sets of visitors to the farm. The first consisted of the men who brought the threshing machine and left it there for work the next morning. They had arrived at about 3.30 and left on their bicycles at 4.30. They were able to be precise about this second timing because a 'buzzer', which always went off at that time to signal a break from work for the farm hands, was heard as they pushed their bicycles along the cinder track.

The men who had brought the threshing-machine did not see Mrs Dobson at the farm, nor did they see her as they made their way down to the main road and into Wolviston. On Teeside in 1938 cycling was the usual means of getting about or getting to work. For other occasions, there was the Billingham-Hartlepool bus service but the age of car ownership for ordinary people was still twenty or even thirty years in the future. The nation travelled by BSA rather than Austin Morris. Bicycles were commonly used for work and, with dropped handlebars, for the weekly Sunday outings of local cycling clubs. This common usage was to be important in the investigation of Mrs Dobson's murder.

On the morning of the day of the murder, Mr Dobson had been to Sedgefield market and had bought eight pigs. The pigs were brought to High Grange Farm by two men in a Bedford truck at about 5.30 p.m. Mr Dobson thought it might have been about ten minutes earlier but he was not sure. Neither Percy Swales, the driver of the Bedford truck, nor his mate Thomas Nelson, saw Mrs Dobson.

Henry Dobson's evidence, as he gave it to Superintendent Kirkup, was that he and his wife had had tea at about 3.15. She had eaten a sandwich of boiled beef, which was the food found in her stomach at the post-mortem examination. If the pathologist and Mr Dobson were both correct, Mrs Dobson died at about 3.45. According to Mr Dobson, however, his wife did not leave the farm until 4.30 and he remembered this because it was getting 'pretty dark'. The most probable explanation was that they had eaten their tea later than he recalled, perhaps close to 4 p.m. The men who had brought the threshing machine left at 4.30 and did not pass Mrs Dobson on the cinder track, presumably because she was still at the farm.

One problem of the investigation was that Mr Dobson remained confused about the timing of events on that afternoon. When giving evidence, he suggested that the threshing machine arrived at 5 p.m., while Bertram Smith and his men who had brought it insisted that they had brought it at 3.30 and had heard the 4.30 'buzzer' as they left. Mr Dobson confused the evidence further when he recalled that his wife went out just after the arrival of the machine, but he thought that was just after 5 p.m. Indeed, he said, his wife had gone out just before the pigs arrived in the Bedford truck.

The truth was that Mr Dobson had been far too busy that afternoon to keep his eye on the clock for timings that he had no reason to suppose would be of the least importance. Taking his evidence in all its forms, it appeared that Mrs Dobson might have left the farm at any time between about 3.50 and 5.10. It would have taken her about ten minutes to walk to the place where her body was found.

It seemed least likely that she had left between 3.50 and 4.30. Mr Dobson thought they had tea at 3.15, giving a time of death – according to the state of digestion – at about 4 p.m. But he also remembered it was getting 'pretty dark' when his wife left, which it would not have been until shortly before 5 p.m. If he was wrong about the time of the meal, or if Mrs Dobson's digestion was imperfect, then the likely time for her leaving the farm was, at the outside, 4.40 to 5.10. This would be supported indirectly by the evidence of the men who brought the threshing machine and who left at 4.30.

Mr Dobson's other contribution was a memory of his wife leaving just before the pigs were brought in the Bedford truck. Superintendent Kirkup established that the truck had left Sedgefield, ten miles away, at 5 p.m. It would probably cover this distance and negotiate the five hundred yard cinder track in time to arrive at the farm by 5.30 or a few minutes before. This was the most important fragment of information because it seemed that the driver and his mate were the only two witnesses who almost certainly saw Mrs Dobson's murderer.

The Bedford truck turned off the A19 road to Billingham and began its progress through the darkness, whining in low gear along the cinder track towards the farm. As it turned on to the track, the driver and his mate saw a man in the beam of the headlights, about fifty yards from the main road. He was standing to the right of the track, in profile, his hands above his head. Though it was dark and their view was not the best, Percy Swales and Thomas Nelson described the man as wearing what appeared to be a blue smock, a brown coloured coat, breeches and gaiters. He was wearing a labourer's cap and seemed to be about thirty years old. At that moment, the man dropped out of sight, upon the earth of the ploughed field to the right-hand side of the cinder track.

The Bedford truck drove on slowly. When it reached the point where the man had been standing to the right, there was a bicycle lying on the ground to the left. The front wheel and handlebars were on the grass verge but the rear wheel was lying on the cinder track. It was black and appeared to have black handlebars. Percy Swales had to pull the wheel of the lorry over to the right to avoid it, feeling as he did so that the truck's rear wheel had gone over the grass verge. As he pulled to the right, Swales made out the figure of a man lying on the ploughed earth of the field but could not see his face clearly. Swales stopped and shouted, 'Hullo! What's the game here?' The man replied, 'I'm all right. I've had one drop over the nine. Drive on.' Swales could hear that the man had a local accent, which was scarcely surprising, and added that he spoke in a firm voice. 'My lights were not actually on him,' Swales told the police. 'I could just see the faint outline of a man lying on the ground, and I drove on to the farm.'

When the two men reached the farm, Percy Swales, still annoyed over the matter of the bicycle on the path and the drunk lying in the field, told one of Mr Dobson's men. 'There is a bicycle lying on the roadway, and I very nearly ran over it, and the man lying in the plough there says he is drunk.' Mr Dobson's farm-hand replied that the man could not be from the farm because 'none of our men are out of the place'.

Nothing more was said about the matter. About quarter of an hour later, when the pigs had been unloaded in the yard, Swales and Nelson set off in the Bedford truck down the cinder track to the main road. There was no sign of the man, and the bicycle had gone. Next morning, at the scene of Mrs Dobson's murder, the track of the Bedford's rear wheel was found on the grass verge, immediately above the point where the body lay. The only reason why Swales had not seen the body at 5.30 was that the verge concealed it or, perhaps, that it was not yet there. The man in the field, who said that he had had 'one drop over the nine', was either lying within a

foot or two of the body or possibly lying on it to conceal it. As
the trial judge was to say, that man 'doubtless was the
murderer'.

There seemed no question that Mrs Dobson was still at the
farm when the threshers left at 4.30, one of the few certain
times which could be established by the sounding of the
'buzzer' for the men to take a break from work. It seemed
equally certain that she was dead by 5.25. Perhaps at the
latest, she left the farm at about 5.10, encountered her
assailant at about 5.20 and was dead before the Bedford truck
stopped at 5.25 or 5.30. If Mr Dobson was also correct that it
was 'pretty dark' when she left, regardless of the time, that
would further reduce the possibility to between lighting-up
time at 4.45 and the latest moment at 5.10. The timings which
Henry Dobson gave were, for understandable reasons,
confused and confusing, but the evidence of other witnesses
was more precise.

There remains, of course, the possibility that Mrs Dobson
had been dead for more than a few minutes when her killer
was caught in the beam of the headlights. How long he might
have stood beside the body no one could say. It is possible, if
she died just before 5 p.m., that he had been standing by the
body for almost half an hour, dismayed by what he had done
and wondering how to save himself. There is no evidence of
this, but it may have happened. At all events, the arrival of
the truck and the fear that he had been identified by its
occupants were enough to put him to flight.

From the evidence of what had occurred on that afternoon,
Superintendent Kirkup had enough to begin his hunt. He
was looking for a local man, aged about thirty, the owner of a
black bicycle with dropped handlebars that were also black.
The man had been wearing a cap, a blue smock, brown
jacket, leggings and gaiters. He had been at High Grange
Farm at least between 5.20 and 5.30, perhaps from 4.45 until
5.30. There had been no sign of him or his bicycle when the
threshers left at 4.30. Despite the inability of the truck-driver
and his mate to make out the man's face, his motives and his
movements might yet be enough to hang him.

3

Superintendent Kirkup soon found a likely suspect. On the evening of 19 January, at about 6 p.m., the day after the murder and some eight hours after the discovery of Mrs Dobson's body, a young man was observed to be behaving rather oddly outside a newsagent's shop at Haverton Hill on the northeast fringe of Billingham where the industrial conurbation began. His name was Robert Hoolhouse, twenty years old, and he worked as a casual labourer, signing on at the labour exchange. Sometimes he worked with Bertram Smith and the threshers, though not when they had gone to Grange Hill Farm. He lived with his parents at Haverton Hill. His girlfriend at the time lived in Wolviston, the village about a mile north of the cinder track to High Grange Farm on the A19. Wolviston and Haverton Hill were at opposite diagonal corners of a square, northwest and southeast. The distance between them was four miles or so, and the journey could be made more or less equally round two opposite sides of the square from Wolviston, either south and then east, or east and then south. On his bicycle, it took Robert Hoolhouse about twenty minutes either way, and a policeman later pedalled the route to verify this.

On the evening of 19 January, Hoolhouse was seen by several people outside the newsagent's shop in Haverton Hill, where the placards announced that a Wolviston woman had been murdered. The first witness was Arthur Nicholson, a postman who arrived at 5.50 p.m. to empty the pillar-box against which Hoolhouse was leaning. They discussed the murder on the placards and Hoolhouse said that he was just going to buy a paper to read about it. He was seen there at approximately 6 p.m. by Bertram Smith who, with his men, had taken the threshing machine to High Grange Farm the previous afternoon. Hoolhouse had not been there. Indeed, he had not even been told where the threshing machine would be.

Smith saw Hoolhouse 'noticing the placards' outside the newsagent's. Smith also saw 'a number of scratches' on the young man's right cheek. 'He appeared to be in a nervous condition, different from usual. I asked him why he had not come on Tuesday [to inquire about work], and he said he had been up to the village. I asked him about the scratches, how he got them, and he said he had fallen off his bicycle at Stevenson's Farm between Cowpen and Haverton Hill. I do not remember if he said when. He said he had fallen over the handlebars. He said it was on Tuesday · but I cannot remember if he said what time. He said he had hurt his shoulder at the same time.'

Smith also thought that Hoolhouse looked pale and shaky. He said to him, 'You look as if you have had a shock.' Hoolhouse replied, 'Yes, and it will be a bit before I get over it.' Smith said something about the murder and Hoolhouse mumbled a reply which the thresher could not hear.

The next person to see and speak to Hoolhouse outside the newsagent's was an ex-policeman, Herbert Collins. He thought the young man looked pale and uneasy. Collins also noticed some abrasions on his face and Hoolhouse told him that he had come off his bicycle on his way to work in the morning. He had put the front brake on too quickly, a common cause of such accidents, and had come off over the handlebars.

Collins asked Hoolhouse if he had been in Wolviston the night before and Hoolhouse agreed that he had been there at about 7 p.m. He had gone by one bus and back on the next. Collins then said that he himself had been interviewed by the police about the murder and that they would be interviewing Hoolhouse too. 'I bloody well hope not,' Hoolhouse said, adding that he could account for his movements. 'I hope you can,' Collins said.

The fourth man who saw Hoolhouse outside the newsagent's was James Fulcher. He did not speak to Hoolhouse and merely overheard his conversation with Smith, though he described the young man as mumbling. 'I heard Hoolhouse say, "The only time I was in Wolviston was about seven o'clock." He meant in the evening. He said he went by one bus and back by the next. Then Mr Smith asked about the scratches on his face. I saw the scratches. He said he had fallen off his bicycle near Stevenson's Farm – put the brake on sharply and fell over the handlebars. He said at first it happened in the morning about eight o'clock. Later he said it happened at dinner time. He said he was in Wolviston at one o'clock and he fell off going there. That was the day we were talking to him, the 19th.'

As for the previous day, that of the murder, it was certainly true that Hoolhouse had been to Wolviston by bus at 7 p.m. and had come back on the next bus. He had gone to meet Dorothy Lax and they had come back to Billingham. They went to the second house at the cinema, where they saw *Under Two Flags*. Afterwards he put Dorothy Lax on the bus for Wolviston and caught a bus himself for Haverton Hill. He was home at about 10.45.

Though he said nothing about it outside the newsagent's, Hoolhouse had also been to see Dorothy Lax and her aunt at Wolviston on the afternoon of the murder, something which he never denied. But at the time of his conversations with the other witnesses, the only public information on the time of the murder was the inaccurate newspaper report which said that Mrs Dobson had last been seen getting off a bus at Wolviston soon after 11 p.m. on 18 January. In fact, she had been dead for about six hours by then. In the light of the report, however, it was not surprising that an innocent man would have given some account of his movements during the evening rather than during the afternoon when he would have assumed, from the newspaper report, that she was still alive.

But there was one other fact which the witnesses mentioned to him. Perhaps it had already caused him to look uneasy. They reminded him that five years earlier he and his family had worked for the Dobsons. With this in mind and having seen how he now behaved, Bertram Smith and Herbert Collins went to the police that night and told them of the odd way in which Hoolhouse seemed to act outside the newsagent's. Superintendent Kirkup would have interviewed the young man in due course, but he now learned something else from Mr Dobson. Hoolhouse had not merely worked at High Grange Farm five years before as a lad of fifteen. He had lived in a cottage there with his parents until there had been a disagreement, after which the family had been dismissed from their employment and turned out of their cottage. It seemed the young man had reason to feel a grudge or resentment, perhaps sufficient to motivate revenge. Superintendent Kirkup decided not to take the risk of leaving matters until the next day. At 1 a.m. on 20 January, a policeman arrived at the home of the Hoolhouses in Haverton Hill. The young man was roused from sleep, told to get dressed and informed that he was being taken to Haverton Hill police station. The police refused to tell him why. Innocent or guilty, it was agreed by his interrogators that he did not seem at his best.

Although he was cautioned at the police station, Hoolhouse agreed to make a statement as to his movements on 18 and 19 January. He had left Haverton Hill at 12.30 p.m. on 18 January and cycled to Wolviston. He visited Dorothy Lax and her aunt Beatrice Husband, remaining with them until about 3.30. He then cycled home by the Cowpen road – east and south – which would not have taken him past or near High Grange Farm, arriving home just after 4 p.m. He left again at 6.30 by bus for Billingham and changed buses for Wolviston. He collected Dorothy Lax, took her to the cinema, put her on a bus for Wolviston afterwards and caught his own bus to Haverton Hill.

The statement, if true, offered an alibi for a time before Mrs Dobson's death. But Hoolhouse cannot have imagined the police would take it at face value. It was established that he had been in the Blue Bell at Newton Bewley, a mile or so northeast of Wolviston, from about 1.45 to 2.45 p.m. on the afternoon of the murder. He had a glass of beer and a small bottle of King's Ale. At 3.10, on his way to Wolviston, he met a friend named Ronald Baldry, an AA patrol man. They went to Wolviston together and arrived at 3.35, a time that could be verified because Baldry had to enter his arrival on his time sheet. On the way to Wolviston, they talked about girls, their usual topic of conversation. Hoolhouse said he was going to visit a girl and might get 'a bit of dick' if her mother was out. But this was the facetious hope that one young man might mention to another rather than the vow of a man prepared, if necessary, to satisfy himself by the rape and murder of an old lady of sixty-seven.

However, Baldry's evidence made nonsense of Hoolhouse's statement that he had visited Dorothy Lax and Beatrice Husband, leaving them at 3.30. He did not even arrive in Wolviston until 3.35. When the police checked the statement with Dorothy Lax and her aunt, the times for the afternoon visit tallied with Baldry's evidence. The two women remembered Hoolhouse arriving at about 3.30 and leaving at 4.30 or 4.40. Hoolhouse conceded that he had got the time wrong but insisted that the statement was otherwise correct. His father, when questioned, remembered him getting home at about 5 p.m., which would correspond with leaving Wolviston at 4.40 on the twenty-minute cycle ride. A neighbour remembered seeing him walk from the coal-shed to the house at Haverton Hill between 4.30 and 5 p.m., presumably very close to the latter time.

If Hoolhouse had murdered Mrs Dobson, his first incorrect statement did nothing to strengthen an alibi. Indeed, it would have given him time to get home at 4 p.m. and return to commit the crime. In the less likely event of Mrs Dobson having died half an hour after a 3.15 tea, it was the other witnesses rather than his first statement which gave him an unbreakable alibi.

As it happened, it was the latter part of the afternoon for which he truly needed an account of his movements. The threshers, leaving High Grange Farm at 4.30, saw no sign of him as they made their way to Wolviston. This suggested that he could not have left the village until after 4.40 if he had, after all, cycled towards the farm. He, of course, insisted that he had gone home the other way. Bertram Smith and his men not only knew Hoolhouse but were his workmates. It was inconceivable that twenty-four hours later, with the news of the murder in their minds and with Smith having reported his odd behaviour outside the newsagent's, not one of them would remember seeing him if he had been on the road from Wolviston to the farm between 4.30 and 4.40.

If Hoolhouse was lying about his route home at 4.40, and if Mrs Dobson left the farm at 4.30 or soon afterwards, he might conceivably have seen her as he cycled past the farm, stopped, raped and murdered her, got back on his bike and reached home within twenty minutes of leaving Wolviston. But the cycle journey alone took that length of time. And there is a stronger objection to this version of the murder. If Hoolhouse had committed the crime at about 4.45, who was the figure seen by two men in the Bedford truck, standing by the body at 5.30? If Hoolhouse was the murderer, it was surely he.

But if that figure was Hoolhouse, who had reached home at 5 p.m., according to his father and a neighbour, he must have left home again almost as soon as he arrived and ridden straight to High Grange Farm. Why? Whatever his feelings towards Mrs Dobson, he could not have known she would be walking down the cinder track at about 5.20 p.m. If he had any business at the farm or with the threshers, surely he would have gone there from Wolviston on his way home. After all, he had come home to change, wash, shave, have a meal and get ready to take Dorothy Lax to the cinema. But within a minute or two of arriving home, he must have left and ridden at top speed to the farm and raped and murdered the old lady at once, in order to be seen in the headlight beam of the Bedford truck at 5.30 or a few minutes before.

The men in the Bedford truck described the unidentified man as wearing a blue smock, a brown coat, leggings and gaiters and a cap. Three witnesses agreed that on his afternoon visit to Wolviston, Hoolhouse was wearing a light-coloured Burberry mackintosh, blue overalls, and brown trousers. They disagreed as to whether he was wearing a cap or a trilby. It was probably a cap. He was certainly not wearing leggings and gaiters, though he might have had a cycle clip on the left leg of his trousers. One other witness thought he was wearing a brown suit under his overalls. Both the cap and the blue overalls were, though not universal, the common dress of labourers. The men in the truck had only an indistinct view of the suspect at 5.30. Perhaps a cycle clip might give the impression of a man wearing breeches and gaiters but that was far from certain. Overalls might be mistaken for a smock. A light coloured mackintosh, however, would scarcely look like a brown coat. Had Hoolhouse, if he was the man, discarded his mackintosh at that point? Making allowances for what might be seen in the darkness, the clothes might have resembled those worn by Hoolhouse that afternoon, but by strict description they were certainly not his. His age was also wrong by ten years.

Whatever the effect of the mistake in his first statement, the evidence of others suggested it was extremely difficult, if not impossible, for Hoolhouse to have been at High Grange Farm when Mrs Dobson died. The most damning evidence against him so far was his behaviour outside the newsagent's. Might not that be explained by his discovery that a woman who had employed him and with whom his family had experienced a bitter quarrel had been murdered twenty minutes from his home? If the police questioned him, he might very well feel that motivation made him a principal suspect. When told that he would probably be questioned, it was understandable that he thought, 'I bloody well hope not.' Would a guilty man have said those words publicly?

Those who saw him on the evening of 18 January and the afternoon of the following day, when the murder had not yet been reported, found him normal in his behaviour. Nor, on the evening of 18 January, did any witness who saw him notice scratches or abrasions on the right hand side of his face. To those who had arrested him he seemed the most likely suspect, because he was the only suspect. Yet he had no record of violence or crime of any sort. It was admitted that he was of previous 'exemplary' character. If he cherished a hatred of the Dobsons, he had certainly never shown it.

If Hoolhouse could not have been at High Grange Farm when Mrs Dobson died, there was an end of the matter. But to prove this beyond any doubt, when the time of the murder could not be precisely given, might be difficult. There was still, of course, the matter of forensic evidence. What was the strength of that? It would surely need to be very persuasive to convict him as the old lady's murderer.

4

The forensic evidence related to four items. There was a penknife in his possession which, like thousands of others, could have been the murder weapon. There was the print of a heel close to the body. There were hairs, including pubic hairs, on the front of his shirt. Finally, there were traces of blood on his clothing and, of course, the abrasions on his face.

The penknife was examined. Its blade was half an inch wide and two and one-eighth inches long. There was a 'very minute' trace of blood in the thumb-nail groove by which the blade was opened. Dr Cookson could not confirm that it was human blood. It might well have been Hoolhouse's blood. After all, he was a farm labourer. By the nature of his work he was likely to sustain a minor or superficial cut from time to time. The knife was taken to pieces but no blood was found in the crevices where it might have remained if the knife was the murder weapon, even though the blade and handle were cleaned. Like hundreds of pocket-knives in the area, this one matched the dimensions of the murder weapon, but that was all that could be said.

As for the print of a man's heel, Detective Sergeant Foster had examined the cast and compared it with Hoolhouse's shoes. When asked whether he could find any 'resemblance between the cast and the accused's shoes,' he replied, 'I certainly could not.' This was in part because the print in the soil was not detailed enough for accurate comparison. As Sergeant Foster put it, 'I would not say that it was the accused's footprint or that it was not, because I cannot say there is any definite mark of resemblance to compare them.' The print of a heel proved nothing either way.

Frederick Gerald Tryhorn, Professor of Chemistry at University College, Hull, was given samples of hair from Hoolhouse and Mrs Dobson to compare with those taken from the suspect's clothes. He found a single hair on Hoolhouse's handkerchief. It was not Hoolhouse's and might, or might not, have been Mrs Dobson's. Professor Tryhorn had been given three or four hairs from Mrs Dobson's head but these differed among themselves. There was also pubic hair on Dobson's shirt which might have been Mrs Dobson's – or might not. When asked if he would be prepared to swear 'that any of these hairs had come from any particular source', Professor Tryhorn said, 'No, I would not.' Asked whether such identification of hairs was not terribly difficult, he said, 'I think it is impossible.'

The evidence of the pubic hair was inconclusive. However, so far as the assault on Mrs Dobson was concerned, there was another factor which would suggest that Hoolhouse was not the man. The victim was described as matted with the semen of her assailant. Yet the clothes Hoolhouse had been wearing, including the front of the shirt, showed no trace of semen whatever. To this point, the scientific evidence was no more damning in the case of Robert Hoolhouse than it might have been in the case of a hundred other men. There remained the abrasions and the bloodstains.

No witness remembered seeing the scratches or abrasions on the right-hand side of Hoolhouse's face before the encounter outside the newsagent's in Haverton Hill at about 6 p.m. on 19 January, twenty-four hours after the murder. The marks were described then and subsequently as being three almost parallel scratches between the cheek-bone and mouth, but they were only three-quarters of an inch long.

Unfortunately there was no scientific evidence as such on the appearance of the marks, merely the opinion of PC Crossley who wrote down Hoolhouse's statement. They were very trivial marks, though Crossley could see them from a distance of twelve inches. He thought they would not have been caused by Hoolhouse falling off his bicycle, but he was in no real position to say. He also examined the bicycle for signs of damage but found none. He admitted, however, that there would have been none if it had fallen on grass.

No one who saw Hoolhouse on the day of the murder remembered seeing marks on his face. Beatrice Hubbard had not seen them. Dorothy Lax, who sat on his right on the bus, had not seen them. When Hoolhouse was charged with murder, no other person came forward to say that the marks were there on 18 January.

There is no doubt, however, that Hoolhouse made matters worse for himself at the police station by changing the story he had told outside the newsagent's and saying that he had fallen off his bicycle on his way home on 18 January rather than on the following day. So far as the murder was concerned it made absolutely no difference, though it made him seem to be a liar. It was suggested that he changed this detail of his story because he believed the erroneous newspaper report that Mrs Dobson was murdered late at night on 18 January and he hoped to show that he had the scratches before then. Once again, it was the witnesses rather than Hoolhouse himself who protected him best. If they were right that the marks were not there on the evening of 18 January, then those marks had nothing to do with the murder. Guilty or innocent, however, there seemed no question that Hoolhouse was scared and confused, having been woken in the middle of the night and taken off for a police interrogation as a suspect killer.

There was a further query, in any case, as to whether Mrs Dobson could have inflicted such marks. When her body was found, she was still wearing the woollen gloves which she had put on at the farm. Could she have scratched Hoolhouse, to the extent that the marks showed, while wearing woollen gloves? There was at least some doubt in the matter. Dr Cookson said that his secretary had put on woollen gloves to see if she could leave marks on Superintendent Kirkup's face. They decided that she could, though they did not actually try the experiment. It was something less than a conclusive demonstration. Once again, the case against Hoolhouse came far short of conclusive proof but did not absolutely dispel suspicion.

The bloodstains were the most contentious issue. There were smears of blood on his handkerchief; drops on his shirt cuffs, described as a blob and three or four little droplets on the right cuff and a few droplets on the left; there were a few spots on his other clothes and one on his cap. When Hoolhouse was questioned about this during the night of his arrest, he said that he had cut himself slightly while shaving, before going out to meet Dorothy Lax on the evening of 18 January. The blood on his handkerchief had come from the aftermath of a boil.

The smears of blood on the other clothing and cap were so tiny that it was impossible for Dr Gerald Lynch, Senior Official Analyst to the Home Office, to establish any blood grouping. He also added that the marks could have been 'up to two or three months old'. This recalled the fact that Hoolhouse was a manual labourer, working with farm implements. It might have seemed remarkable if, over a period of two or three months, he had not suffered some scratch or graze sufficient to leave the minute quantity of blood found on his clothing.

This left the blood on the shirt cuffs and handkerchief as the only evidence of likely significance. Hoolhouse insisted that he had cut himself while shaving soon after 5 p.m. on the evening of 18 January. A few spots had got on to his shirt cuffs. The shirt was brown and perhaps he did not see the spots at the time. He shaved with his collar turned in, to avoid getting lather on it, so the cuffs were the only part on which blood had spotted or been smeared.

No one noticed a cut on his face but it seemed that he might have nicked a pimple, which would have bled without leaving an obvious cut. It would leave what Dr Lynch called 'a tiny little spot' on the skin of the face for some time afterwards. There is no indication, however, that anyone looked for 'a tiny little spot'.

The handkerchief was examined. Though there were smears of blood on it, there was no evidence of pus, which would have indicated that the blood had come from a boil.

Hoolhouse could not establish that the blood on his shirt

cuffs came from a cut while shaving and it seemed that he was either mistaken or lying about the blood on his handkerchief having come from a boil. The amounts of blood, of course, were tiny. And if that was all, it was surely not enough to hang him. Apart from the forensic evidence, it might seem next to impossible that he could have been at High Grange Farm when Mrs Dobson died, in which case the source of the drops of blood was immaterial. The evidence of pubic hairs on his shirt counted for little in the complete absence of semen. The heel print was not identified as his. As for the penknife, there was nothing to link it to the murder beyond its general appearance. As the judge said to the trial jury, 'It is a knife such as some of you may have exactly the same in your own pockets.'

A more general point in the suspect's favour was also to be made by the judge. 'Nothing that is known to have belonged to the deceased woman is found upon this man. Nothing that is known to have belonged to this man is found upon or near the deceased woman.'

In deciding what action to take in respect of Hoolhouse, the authorities now faced two questions: Was it possible beyond reasonable doubt that Hoolhouse could have been at the farm when Mrs Dobson died? It would require a scarcely believable degree of coincidence, split-second timing, and probably an inexplicable urge to leave home again the moment he got there. There was no evidence at all for any of these requirements.

If he could have been at the farm, despite all this, did the forensic evidence suggest beyond reasonable doubt that he was the murderer? There was no aspect of it which linked him beyond reasonable doubt with the crime. Indeed, the absence of semen on the shirt suggested strongly that he was not the assailant.

It was agreed that he was a young man of good character. Against this might be set the motive of revenge against the Dobsons who had turned his family out of the cottage five years earlier. There was also his behaviour outside the newsagent's. Yet these two things might equally well be linked in his favour. He guessed that he would be a suspect, on the basis of such a possible motive, and the prospect of an ordeal at the hands of the police made him uneasy. Hoolhouse was a casual labourer, not a bright, fluent, and

articulate young man. His statement was written for him by
PC Crossley. He was understandably in awe of the web of
circumstance in which he was caught.

To the dismay of Hoolhouse himself and to the surprise of
others, he was now charged with the murder of Margaret
Dobson.

5

It was at this point that things began to go badly wrong. He
was asked to take a blood test and he refused. It had been
established that the blood on his shirt and handkerchief was
Group II – later known as Type A. This was the group to
which Mrs Dobson belonged, as did 42% of the population.
A larger group was Group IV – later Type 0 – to which 47% of
the population belonged. If it proved that Hoolhouse, like
Mrs Dobson, was Group II, then his story of having cut
himself while shaving might still be true but not beyond
doubt. If, however, he was found to belong to another group,
then he must be lying about cutting himself.

Hoolhouse refused to take a blood test, which he was
absolutely entitled to do. By now, if he was innocent, he had
every reason to be alarmed about the way in which a case
against him was being constructed by the police from the
flimsiest of components. He was perhaps unwilling or
frightened of further cooperation. Possibly he was advised
not to take the test because, in the face of so weak a case, he
did not need to give his antagonists further ammunition.

Forensically, Hoolhouse had little to gain and everything
to lose from a blood test. It would do little to establish his
innocence, though it might suggest his guilt. If he was Group
II, like Mrs Dobson, he could still be her murderer. If he was
not Group II, then the blood on his cuffs and handkerchief
was not his. Suspicion would be strengthened to accusation,
even to proof, of murder. For whatever reason, he refused
the test. The case against him appeared so uncertain that
before the magistrates, on 16 February, his solicitor
demanded that he should be released on bail. This was
refused.

The case came to trial at Leeds Assizes on 28 March 1938
and lasted for three days. Paley Scott KC, for the Crown,

described it as 'a case of very much less evidence than one usually finds'. Indeed, the prosecution case was so weak that at the end of it Arthur Morley KC, defending Hoolhouse, submitted that there was no case for the defence to answer. 'I venture to suggest that the prosecution's case here is: Assume the guilt of the accused and look how many little pieces of evidence are consistent with his guilt. My Lord, that is a complete inversion of the methods and principles which are usually adopted in criminal trials.'

The defence submitted that there was no convincing evidence that Hoolhouse was or could have been at High Grange Farm. There was not one item among the forensic evidence which necessarily linked him with the murder. That a young man of twenty, of exemplary character, would suddenly rape an old lady of sixty-seven and then murder her stretched belief beyond its limits. If the case went to the jury on such evidence, Hoolhouse was really being required to prove his innocence. Such a requirement was repugnant to the very basis of English criminal law. The burden of proof lay on the prosecution. Unless they could show beyond reasonable doubt that Hoolhouse was guilty, he was entitled to an acquittal. They had failed to show that, even before the defence began. The case should therefore be withdrawn from the jury.

Mr Justice Wrottesley listened to the defence submission. 'I must say at once,' he remarked when Arthur Morley had finished, 'that this is essentially a case for the jury to decide.'

The defence had elected to present no evidence. Neither Robert Hoolhouse nor any other witness would be called. It seemed unnecessary. Perhaps, indeed, Arthur Morley had expected the trial to end, after his submission, with the withdrawal of the case from the jury. He was to be disappointed. By calling no witnesses, however, he enjoyed the advantage of having the last word to the jury, following Paley Scott's closing address for the Crown.

The prosecution case was that Mrs Dobson had been murdered soon after 4.30, that Hoolhouse had left Wolviston at about 4.30, ridden past the farm, raped and murdered the old lady fifty yards from the main road, and then continued home. The first objection to this was that Bertram Smith and his threshers would have seen him as they pushed their bicycles down the cinder track at 4.30 and then rode down the A19 to Wolviston, arriving at about 4.40. The second objection was that even if Hoolhouse left Wolviston immediately at 4.40, he had just enough time to arrive home by 5 p.m. but no time to stop and commit a rape and murder. Paley Scott told the jury that there was no evidence as to the time when Hoolhouse reached home. That was true, in the sense that no witness had been called by the defence during the trial. But both the father, Frederick Hoolhouse, and a neighbour, Doris Teale, had given evidence to the police that the young man was home by 5 p.m. There was another weakness in the prosecution hypothesis. Even if Hoolhouse had murdered Mrs Dobson at about 4.45 p.m., why was he standing by the body when the Bedford truck arrived at 5.30? He had come home to change his clothes, which witnesses saw he had done, wash, shave, have his tea, and go out at 6.30 to meet Dorothy Lax. There is no evidence that he rode back to the farm as well, nor did the prosecution suggest it.

Two points about the police interrogation of Hoolhouse emerged from Arthur Morley's closing address. First, he pointed out that Hoolhouse had gone to the police station in the very same clothes, including shirt and handkerchief, in which it was alleged he had committed the murder. Surely a guilty man would have got rid of such evidence or at least put on a clean shirt?

A second point concerned the first statement made to the police when Hoolhouse claimed to have been in Wolviston an hour earlier than he was on 18 January. He had been in Wolviston earlier, but that had been on 19 January. The police had asked for an account of his movements on both days. The press report had erroneously described Mrs Dobson as still being alive after 11 p.m. on 18 January. Roused from sleep and questioned in the middle of the night, an innocent and possibly confused man might have given his movements for the afternoon of 19 January. After all, so far as he knew – if he was innocent – his movements on 18 January were unimportant until after 11 p.m. Arthur Morley concluded, 'The prosecution, in my submission, is able to present to you a series of vague theories, all unproved, and you are asked to convict a man of unblemished character, quite a sober man, of the most serious crime known to the law.'

Mr Justice Wrottesley summed up. He warned the jury

that it was not enough, 'if you should think that very probably the prosecution have got the right man'. Because the defence had not called witnesses to prove Hoolhouse's arrival home by 5 p.m., it was not evidence. But even without that, allowing the possibility that Hoolhouse might have been at the farm at 5.30, the judge concluded, 'this only establishes, not that he did do the murder, but that he might have done it … that is not enough in itself.' As for Hoolhouse's conduct outside the newsagent's the next day, 'it appears to me to be very dangerous that a jury should rely on another man's account of a man's demeanour.'

In the forensic evidence, it would have seemed 'a little surprising' if Mrs Dobson had been able to scratch her assailant's face while wearing woollen gloves. As for the blood grouping, Hoolhouse was completely within his rights in refusing to take a blood test. Even had he taken the test and had he been proved to have lied about cutting himself shaving because his blood was not Group II, 'it still does not establish that this man murdered that woman.' In conclusion, the prosecution 'have got a number of things in regard to each one of which, when you test it, it amounts to no more than this, that it is quite consistent with this man having committed the murder: but it is consistent with his not having committed it.' If the jurors thought, 'that very likely that young fellow did it, but we cannot be certain – if that is the frame of mind you are left in, then your duty is equally plain, and it is to say "Not Guilty".'

Few of those who heard the evidence and the summing up doubted that Hoolhouse would be acquitted. The jury was out for four hours and twenty minutes. They brought in a verdict of 'Guilty'. Robert Hoolhouse was sentenced to death.

6

Hoolhouse waited in the condemned cell of Durham Gaol for six weeks until his appeal was heard on 9 May. The appeal was dismissed. The Court of Appeal held that the trial judge had been correct in overruling the defence submission that there was no case to answer. On the point that the summing up had not stressed that if Hoolhouse was home at

5 p.m. he could not have committed the murder, the appeal
judges found that his arrival home was not 'evidence before
the court'.

The news that the appeal had been dismissed caused
considerable misgiving on Teeside. A petition with almost
15,000 signatures urged the Home Secretary, Sir Samuel
Hoare, to reprieve Hoolhouse. On 24 May, when he had been
in the condemned cell for two months, Hoolhouse
maintained his innocence and his belief that justice would
not hang an innocent man. On that day, however, Sir Samuel
Hoare announced that he had failed to discover any grounds
for interfering with 'the due course of the law'. Two days
later, Robert Hoolhouse was hanged.

Perhaps he was unlucky in his Home Secretary. Sir Samuel
Hoare had been Foreign Secretary until he was forced from
office by public indignation at his appeasement of Mussolini,
over Abyssinia, in 1935. He was made Home Secretary as a
consolation. How much attention did he give to the case?
The latter half of May 1938 saw the first crisis of the year over
Czechoslovakia, in which Britain and France called Hitler's
bluff, as they would fail to do in the autumn. Sir Samuel
Hoare, like the rest of the cabinet, was too occupied with the
fate of Europe to spare much time for that of one manual
labourer in Durham Gaol.

The Court of Appeal and the Home Secretary had done
nothing for Hoolhouse, but it was the jury which decided his
fate. They had been presented with one of the weakest cases
for the prosecution in any English murder trial. They had
been cautioned by the judge against hasty conviction at
almost every point of the summing up. Why had they found
the defendant guilty?

During their deliberations, they asked to see Hoolhouse's
bicycle and his statement to the police. The significance of
the bicycle may have been that the driver's mate in the
Bedford truck saw a machine with black dropped
handlebars, whereas Hoolhouse's handlebars were silver.
The statement to the police was perhaps more damning. Was
it confusion or deceit that made Hoolhouse give the wrong
time at first for his visit to Wolviston on the afternoon of 18
January? There was no point to any deceit. The incorrect
statement gave him an alibi that was too early, whereas the
truth was more likely to shield him. Moreover, he must have

known that the first thing the police would do would be to check the times with the two young women whom he had visited. It had, of course, been revealed that the statement was written for him as he spoke by PC Crossley. It further emerged that parts of the statement were not volunteered by Hoolhouse but were answers to questions that were put to him. If he was innocent, knowing only what had been wrongly reported in the press about Mrs Dobson being alive at 11 p.m., a phrase like 'the afternoon of the murder' would have meant to him not 18 January but 19 January, when he had indeed visited Wolviston and the two women at an earlier time.

Perhaps he also condemned himself, in the eyes of the jury, by refusing to take a blood test. Most people did not know their blood groups, which were something of a novelty, and it is most unlikely that Hoolhouse would have known his. Was it his own decision that he would not take a test or was it suggested to him that a result showing he was Group II would not prove his innocence, while one showing him to be of any other group might put the rope round his neck?

Was he also the victim of a misjudgment by his defence lawyers? Arthur Morley took a gamble in his submission that there was no case to answer. When the judge ruled that there was, he made it sound more likely to the jurors that Hoolhouse was guilty. Then there was the defence decision to call no evidence. Perhaps Hoolhouse might not have performed well in the witness box and was best kept out of it. However, the decision also meant that two witnesses who could place him at home in Haverton Hill at 5 p.m. on 18 January were not called. Their corroboration was not evidence in the case.

By calling no evidence, Arthur Morley had the last word with the jury, after the closing speech for the prosecution. There might be some advantage in this, but it was lessened by the judge's summing-up which was in itself sympathetic to the defence interpretation of the evidence.

It was for the prosecution to prove the defendant's guilt, not for Hoolhouse to prove his innocence. Was he guilty? At every turn in the case, the answer seemed inconclusive, except in one respect. If he was at Haverton Hill at 5 p.m., even for five minutes, he could not have been at High Grange

Farm between 4.40 and 5.25. Whatever the forensic evidence, whatever the blood groupings or abrasions, whatever the truth of his afternoon visit to Dorothy Lax and Beatrice Husband, if he was not at the farm between those times, he was not the man who killed Margaret Dobson.

4   The Case of the
Diamond-Weave Whip (1946)

1

The late spring of 1946 was a warm and sunny prelude to the first summer of peace. London was still marked by the devastation of the blitz, its walls stencilled with white or yellow signs that directed the inhabitants to Air-Raid Shelters, ARP posts and static water-tanks. Yet the quiet of the summer sky was no longer broken by the ugly stuttering growl and sudden deathly silence of the V2 Flying Bomb or the distant throbbing hum of approaching bomber squadrons. Shortages and rationing continued, but the restaurants and car showrooms of the West End were busy again. It was the summer of demobilization, the last ritual of a great war. The servicemen of the Empire and the United States were in London or Southampton on their way home and British troops were returning from Europe and the Far East. Hotel rooms were fully booked, cinemas and theatres crowded. Charlie Chester and Tommy Handley filled the air-waves with wise-crack wit. The Crazy Gang drew capacity audiences to the Victoria Palace and the Palladium. The nude chorus-girls of the Windmill tantalized men behind a shimmer of ostrich fans.

England's war criminals, men like John Amery or William Joyce, 'Lord Haw-Haw', who had broadcast from Berlin on behalf of the Third Reich, had been tried and hanged a few months before. The trial of the Nazi leaders dragged on at Nuremburg. For most men and women, the massed ranks of the Victory Parade on 8 June, with King George VI taking the salute as the columns marched down the Mall, marked the end of the world's nightmare.

For the first time in almost ten years the people of England felt entitled to a good time without either being told that the clouds were gathering or watching the conflict itself surround them. As the summer began, there was ice-cream again, which had vanished during six years of conflict. Such rarities as oranges and lemons were on general sale. The trains to the coast were crowded, the seaside hotels crammed and the beaches, in the warm weather, taken over at night by those who could find nowhere else to sleep.

In London, black-out had given way to black market or what Superintendent John Gosling called bluntly 'a thieves market'. It was the culture of 'spivs' and 'drones'. The new criminals had been well-trained during military service. They were younger, tougher and more resourceful than the old pre-war 'villains'. Shortages and regulations bred crime. Food and clothing were still rationed. Tobacco and drink carried massive excise duties. Jewellery and luxuries bore a heavy Purchase Tax. Gosling described the result: 'They swooped almost every night. Lorry-loads of tea, sugar, butter, clothes, cigarettes and whisky disappeared from the streets.... Jewellery and cash vanished from private houses into the pockets of thieves who worked like phantoms. Furs and rings, clothing and petrol coupons, carpets, lipsticks, typewriters, razor-blades, shoes – anything with a ready cash value.'

Detective Superintendent Gosling was head of the newly formed 'Ghost Squad' of undercover officers at Scotland Yard. Among its targets was a group of public school ex-officers who were operating a sophisticated cat-burglary racket in the wealthier areas of Knightsbridge and Chelsea. Their social life revolved round the more expensive cocktail bars and clubs, the dinner parties and dance-floors of the new age of peace, private clubs in the Edgware Road and Bayswater where sexual aberrations were catered for and made the source of hard cash. This twilight world offered threats to law and order and induced the Yard to set up the Ghost Squad on 1 January 1946.

By 21 June 1946, the crime figures and the temperatures were riding high. Summer weather had turned the London parks into a lido for girls in sunsuits and their demob-happy escorts. Among those who sought a share of the good things that were to come was a talented young artist and aspiring film-star and novelist, Margery Gardner. She was a new type of young woman who had abandoned her husband and baby in Sheffield and set out to make her fortune alone in bohemian London. So far, she had found little work, except occasionally as a film extra. Apart from her other talents, however, she was sexually adventurous and casually promiscuous. Margery Gardner was known to the police because she had been a passenger in a stolen car some months before. The vehicle was chased by a police car and rammed at Hyde Park Corner. The incident had connected her with that well-heeled underworld of Knightsbridge and Chelsea which had begun to interest the Ghost Squad.

On that sunny afternoon of 21 June, Margery Gardner was lying on a bed in Room 4 of the Pembridge Court Hotel near Notting Hill Gate. The curtains were closed against the sun, leaving the room almost in darkness. She was lying face-down on the bed, naked. Someone had undone the bonds which held her wrists to the corners of the bed-head but her ankles were still pinioned. There were seventeen marks, stripes left by a riding-whip, across her buttocks and her back. Though it was a twin-bedded room, Margery Gardner was alone, and she had been dead for more than twelve hours.

2

A chambermaid had made the discovery of the young woman's body and had called Alice Wyatt, daughter-in-law of the hotel's owner. Mrs Wyatt telephoned Notting Hill Police Station, a few streets away in Ladbroke Grove. Sergeant Fred Averill was on the scene ten minutes later. For the rest of that afternoon, officers and experts of increasing importance arrived at the tall terraced hotel which looked across the central gardens of Pembridge Square. Divisional Chief Inspector Reg Spooner was there from Hammersmith to lead the inquiry. Until three months before, he had been Major Spooner, deputy head of MI5's wartime anti-espionage unit, B57. Scotland Yard's fingerprint expert, Superintendent Fred Cherrill, and his police photographers had already begun to record the scene of Margery Gardner's

death. A growing body of reporters and cameramen gathered
on the pavement of the square.

No one in that room had the least doubt that this was one
of the most lurid and sadistic sex murders of the age. It was a
scene which made people suggest that hanging was too good
for a man who could perpetrate such a crime. Margery
Gardner had been tied down and gagged. She had been
stripped naked and thrashed with a diamond-weave
riding-whip. The atrocity of such an implement used on her
naked buttocks or back was enough to make one wince. To
compound the horror, it seemed she had been penetrated by
the whip.

Her clothes and handbag were still in the room. There
were only a few pence in the bag, because that was all she
possessed. However, there was her wartime identity card by
which Spooner recalled the incident of the stolen car. She
was known as 'Ocelot Margie' in Chelsea's bohemia, a
compliment to the imitation fur coat she sometimes wore.
The other evidence of the killing itself was slight. There were
apparent traces of blood in the washbasin, as if something
had been rinsed there. There was a smear of blood on the
underside of the pillow on the unoccupied bed. The killer
had left no possessions in the room. There was no sign of the
diamond-weave whip. It was obvious that she had been
murdered by a sexual maniac but what, specifically, had she
died of?

The man who could answer that question was in a squad
car, racing towards central London from the Police College at
Hendon, where he had been giving a lecture. Keith Simpson,
Home Office pathologist, arrived at about six o'clock. He
confirmed that Margery Gardner had died soon after
midnight. He was fairly sure, even at this stage, that she had
been suffocated. There was a bruise on her jaw which
suggested that her head had been held and her face pushed
into the pillow. If she had already been tied hand and foot,
and gagged, it would only have required obstruction of her
nostrils to kill her. But most of all, Simpson was intrigued by
the marks of the whip. To Superintendent Tom Barratt of
Scotland Yard, the senior officer present, Simpson said, 'If
you find that whip, you've found your man.' But it was not
forensic expertise, merely humdrum investigation, that was
to track down the unknown assailant.

Spooner discovered that Margery Gardner had lived in a succession of West London hotels and boarding-houses during the previous twelve months. Cromwell Road, Earls Court and Chelsea had all been home to her. Sometimes, having no money for rent, she had stayed with friends and sometimes shared the beds of men she knew. She was a familiar face in such places as the Normandie Hotel near the junction of Knightsbridge and Sloane Street, in the bar and on the dance floor of the Panama Club near South Kensington tube station, in Knightsbridge pubs like the Trevor Arms and the smart little mews cottage of the Nag's Head in Kinnerton Street with its low beams and cosy fire-lit parlour.

At the time of her death, she had a room in Earls Court Square, a short distance from the District and Circle Line station of the underground. She had covered the walls with her own murals. The room was a jumble of millboards and palettes, paintings and sketches, stacked in hope of sale on the boxes, cupboards and chests of drawers. There were sheets of Polyphotos, her self-publicity for the film studios at Ealing or Elstree. She had also decided to try making her living as a novelist. On the table of the room lay an autobiographical novel she was completing. It broke off in a passage of self-description written the night before she died. It seemed an appropriate epitaph. 'She had girl friends, although she got on better with men. She was bold and reckless in those days, finding her feet and her own values – and her mistakes.'

For Chief Inspector Spooner, however, the register of the Pembridge Court Hotel made far more interesting reading. The occupant of Room 4 had entered his name, and that of a companion, upon his arrival a few days before: 'Lt Col & Mrs N G C Heath, Black Hill Cottage, Romsey'.

In response to Spooner's first appeal, a taxi driver was found who had taken two fares to the Pembridge Court Hotel from the Panama Club at about midnight, just before the estimated time of Margery Gardner's death. Harry Harter looked at the young woman's body in Hammersmith Mortuary. He could not be sure that she was the woman in his taxi. Then the Polyphotos from Margery Gardner's room were produced. Yes, said Harter, she was the one. He was shown a man's photograph. That was the man. The couple had been so drunk that they clung to one another as they went up the steps to the front door and the man let them into the hotel with his key.

Spooner had what he wanted. The man's photograph, which Harter identified, was from a confidential file in the Criminal Records Office, CRO No.28142-37. Its subject was Neville George Clevely Heath, by no means unknown to Scotland Yard. Just before six o'clock on the following morning, Spooner sent a top-priority alert to all police districts in England and Wales. Neville Heath was to be found and detained before he could kill again.

3

The CRO file which occupied Spooner until dawn next day was of impressive size. Neville George Clevely Heath was born at Ilford on 6 June 1917, though he spent most of his childhood in the solid middle-class comforts of Merton Hall Road, Wimbledon. Despite his aristocratic pretensions, his father was a barber at Waterloo Station, though the family was descended from the illustrator and engraver James Heath, who had been appointed engraver to George III. Educated first at a convent school and then as a day-boy at the neighbouring public school Rutlish, he was a good athlete and generally popular.

Already, however, there were rumours of tendencies towards sexual violence. His reason for leaving the convent school, it was said, was that he had been left alone with a girl in the classroom and that the teacher had returned to find young Heath thrashing the girl with the classroom cane. There was also an incident at a friend's house when he had indulged in horse-play with a teenage girl, sufficiently alarming to provoke her to hysterics. It was said that Heath had gripped her by the throat to hold her head still while he kissed her and that he left the imprints of his fingers upon her neck. Of the other curiosities in his behaviour, he had a fetish for stealing girls' handkerchiefs. How profound the disturbance might be which manifested itself in these ways was not investigated. Evelyn Walkenden, the Member of Parliament for Doncaster, had a London house near the Heath family. He encountered Neville Heath when the boy was fifteen and concluded, 'An extremely charming lad, also an impossible fantastic liar.'

At sixteen, Heath achieved modest success in his School Certificate and left for a job in a warehouse. He was by now the familiar figure, tall and good-looking, with fair wavy hair and a film-star profile. His good looks and manners, in the 1930s, carried him through almost all difficulties. After a year as a part-time territorial soldier in the Artists Rifles, he joined the Royal Air Force as an officer cadet at the end of 1935, when he was eighteen years old. It was the beginning of a great adventure and also of a life of systematic crime.

After a few months as a cadet at Cranwell, Pilot Officer Heath was posted to RAF Duxford, near Cambridge, in 1936. He did well as a pilot and a year later had been promoted to Flying Officer. His ability as an athlete made him an obvious choice as Duxford's sports officer. He referred casually to his family, his 'people' who had an estate in Suffolk and who made him quite the equal of any other young officer on the station. To judge by the money he spent on girls, cars, and entertainment, no one would have guessed that his father was a railway-station barber.

In March 1937, he was posted to an active service squadron at RAF Mildenhall. He arrived on 20 March. Next morning he vanished, sending an apologetic letter to Squadron Leader Turton-Jones at Duxford, resigning his commission. 'I think this will be the easiest way out to save dragging the name of a decent squadron in the mud.' The cheque for his large final mess bill at Duxford bounced. The accounts now revealed that Neville Heath had been systematically pilfering mess funds as sports officer. It took the RAF Police three months to collect him from Wimbledon and take him to RAF Debden in Essex for court-martial. While there, he broke his parole as an officer, stole an NCO's car and returned to London. He was picked up by the civilian police a few days later.

Though his barrister described the offences as the errors of a 'mere boy', the court-martial sentenced him to be cashiered. The Air Ministry softened this and merely dismissed him from the service. Heath went about telling the story of being dismissed for a dare-devil caper in which he had flown an RAF fighter under the span of a river bridge, for a bet. He had been dismissed for hazarding the safety of his aircraft.

Neville Heath now became, variously, Captain Bruce Lockhart, 'The Cambridge Blue', Captain Selway MC, Lieutenant-Colonel James Robert Cadogan Armstrong, Group Captain Rupert Brooke, Lord Nevill, Lord Dudley, and many more. He was the type of confidence trickster known in the trade as a falcon, one who snares his victim by pretence of rank and breeding. As Lord Jimmy Dudley – Trinity College, Cambridge and c/o The House of Lords – he scattered bogus cheques over Cambridge and East Anglia during 1937. He also sold the car which he had hired. This phase of his career ended with a famous and characteristic exchange in the lounge bar of the Sherwood Inn, Nottingham.

'Excuse me, sir. Are you Lord Dudley?'

'As a matter of fact, old man, I am.'

'Well, I am Inspector Hickman of the Nottingham CID.'

'In that case, old man, I am not Lord Dudley.'

On 11 November 1937, the Nottingham magistrates put him on probation. On 12 July 1938 he was in the dock at the Old Bailey, as well as in the columns of the *Evening Standard*. He had been charged with house-breaking at Edgware, defrauding the Star and Garter hotel at Richmond, stealing a car and cheques at Pevensey Bay, as well as robbing his 'fiancée' of her golf clubs. A number of other charges were not proceeded with. Heath pleaded guilty and this 'ex-public schoolboy and former RAF officer' was sent to Borstal training for a period not exceeding three years.

Long before three years had passed, Heath was released from Hollesley Bay Borstal settlement for war service in September 1939. The RAF refused to have him back, but he joined the Royal Army Service Corps as a private. His charm held good. By the time that he was posted to the Middle East, six months later, he was First Lieutenant Neville Heath, a thief and trickster restored to the rank of officer and gentleman.

For a year, Heath played his part in guarding the oil pipeline from Iraq to Haifa, with frequent periods of leave in Cairo. He was next court-martialled in Jerusalem on 17 and 18 July 1941. He had been charged with fraudulently drawing double pay by having a second pay-book, with obtaining money by dishonoured cheques, and being absent from duty without proper reason. To give good measure, he had also stolen and sold the brigadier's car. For the second time in his life, he was sentenced to be cashiered. This time the sentence was confirmed.

By now there was more to Heath than the con-man of pre-war England. He had always specialized in raising money from the families of girls whose ears he had bitten, to use his own phrase. The method was simple. Turning on the full battery of his charm, Heath would woo the daughter of a reasonably affluent family. They would become engaged. Her family would buy him presents, which he might sell or pawn. He would buy her presents, using worthless cheques. When the truth was revealed – that Heath was simultaneously engaged to a string of these 'fiancées' – there was little the families could do. If Heath came to court, the world would hear how a daughter had been tricked, seduced and probably bedded, by this plausible young crook. Not only had Heath profited by the 'presents' that came his way, but the presents he had given to the girl would naturally be returned to him. As for the bills he had run up, the girl's family would almost certainly pay them rather than see their daughter made a laughing stock.

A cold cruelty ran parallel to Heath's handsome amiability. In the Middle East, according to his adjutant Paull Hill, it was evident for the first time that this cruelty extended to sexual sadism. Heath was known at the Hotel Continental in Cairo and the bar of Shepheards Hotel. Most of those who met him did not see him in conversation with a tout called Sonnie outside the Continental. Sonnie arranged Heath's visits to a brothel run by 'Ibrahim', an establishment with a so-called 'Amazon Room'. The majority of girls who went to bed with him knew nothing of these visits. For £50, Heath might spend the night with two or three girls whom he could undress, tie down and beat with a variety of implements. This was why he needed a second pay-book and a bundle of worthless cheques. This was where he absented himself from duty without good reason. To some companions, including his adjutant who was of equivalent rank, though in the RAF, Heath described the events of such nights. Hill was dismayed, not least by the youth of some of the girls. One pair of sisters, Andrea and Iola, whose mother was Greek, were sixteen and fifteen respectively.

Such was his reputation when Heath was put aboard the

troopship *Mooltan* to be returned in disgrace to England via the Cape. When the ship docked at Durban to take on supplies, the lure of neon-lit hotels and clubs after the London and Cairo black-outs, the warm beaches and resort pleasures, proved too strong. Neville Heath went missing. Captain Selway MC, a young military hero with a limp, appeared in the society of middle-class Durban.

Captain Selway, the wounded hero, gave way to James Robert Cadogan Armstrong, sometimes known as Bill Armstrong, a volunteer for the South African Air Force. He was accepted for pilot training and astonished his instructors by his apparent natural aptitude. In no time, he was an instructor himself.

Heath was something of a catch for the society of the Rand during 1942 and 1943. His stories of aerial combat were vivid and convincing. His good looks and charm were a passport to the parties and drawing-rooms of hostesses to whom he presented himself as the son of Mr and Mrs P.J. Armstrong of Melton Hall, Suffolk. He wore the coveted Hawks Club tie of Cambridge men who have won a double blue – boxing and rugger in this case. He had not been picked for the Boat Race but had rowed at Henley for his college, Trinity. Jimmy – or Bill – Armstrong talked as though he might have done all these things. His good nature and matinée idol looks made his new friends eager to believe him. He was well thought of by prominent figures in South African society, Sir Ernest and Lady Oppenheimer among them.

The darker side of Captain James Robert Cadogan Armstrong's career was reserved for such South African accounts as Benjamin Bennett's, published a decade later. There were stories of Heath having attacked young women whom he was driving home, and even of a nurse whose body was mysteriously found in a burnt-out car after an accident. These may have been the tall tales a murderer sometimes attracts after conviction. In reality, there had been a scandal in a discreet Johannesburg brothel which catered for officers on leave. Heath and a young woman had gone into a room together and the door was locked. There were cries from within, to which no one paid much attention. When the girl was allowed out by Heath, she wore only the shreds of her underwear 'She had been lashed with a cane,' Bennett reported. 'When she tried to protect herself Heath had caught her by the throat, forcing her to the floor and dug his knee into the pit of her stomach.' Holding her over his knee like this, he had stripped and beaten her.

Heath left the house and no report was made to the police. The manageress 'had no wish to encourage too close investigation of her business premises'. On a second occasion, 'Heath tied a young woman to a bed and thrashed her with a buckled belt.' This time, the police were telephoned. But as one person telephoned, others ejected Heath from the building. By the time the police arrived, he was nowhere to be seen. Bennett also cites reports of Heath as 'a voracious reader of pornography and a collector of indecent photographs. Suppliers found him an eager purchaser and could never satisfy his demand for illustrations of sexual aberrations.' In London and Cairo alike, it seems, there were sealed cellophane packets of photographs on display showing either schoolgirls in their early teens being punished by sadistic teachers or naked Middle Eastern women in places of exotic captivity. For the most part, these were amateur theatricals. However, according to Heath's account of Cairo, given to Flight Lieutenant Paull Hill on the *Mooltan*, photographs were taken for sale when unwilling girls were flogged in 'Ibrahim's' Red Room.

One thing was plain. Neville Heath was not a bedroom sadist because he had been seduced by such photographs and books. He collected them because his sadism was long established. Yet there were women in his life towards whom Heath always behaved as the gallant, charming and courteous suitor. In February 1942, despite her wealthy family's disapproval, he eloped with and married Elizabeth Pitt Rivers. Heath was three years younger than his bride. He falsified his age on the marriage certificate, describing himself as thirty-one rather than twenty-four, and he also falsified his name as William Frederick Armstrong. He claimed to have been born in the Orange Free State and to have been an engineer at the Vaal-Hartz Irrigation project in Andalusia. Later that year a son was born to the couple.

In May 1944, Captain Jimmy Armstrong was seconded to RAF Bomber Command for the attack on Europe. He returned to England and, under his *nom de guerre*, was posted to RAF Finmere in Oxfordshire. He flew on active service and, when his plane was damaged over the Rühr, he baled out with his crew and walked to safety. But he also forged and counter-signed his log-books for the benefit of his girlfriends, so that the entries appeared to confirm his repeated acts of cool heroism against near-impossible odds. To the film-star looks and the bedroom sadism there was now added, bizarrely, a dash of Biggles. With the war's end, he was returned to South Africa. By this time, the South African authorities knew his true identity.

On his return to Cape Town, he celebrated by travelling to Durban, where he lived at the Durban Club on the Esplanade. He carried off his imposture by distributing dud cheques and wearing medal ribbons to which he was not entitled – the DFC and the Africa Star. Court-martialled yet again in December 1945, he was dismissed from the service and put on a troopship for England. The Pitt Rivers family paid him off with £2000 and he was divorced by his wife on the grounds of desertion. He arrived in London on 5 February 1946.

On 22 February, Heath had lunch with a young woman of his acquaintance. She is referred to in the police statement as M— B—. Her name was not subsequently disclosed. Conrad Phillips, an *Evening Standard* journalist, later recorded seeing Heath with 'a tall willowy blonde with a chorus girl smile and a thirst for rum and orange'. They had drinks at Oddenino's in Regent Street, lunch at the Berkeley, tea in a friend's flat, drinks in Shepherd Market, more drinks at the Brevet Club and then more drinks in Heath's room on the fifth floor of the Strand Palace Hotel. It was after midnight when a duty electrician heard a woman's voice inside Room 504. 'Stop! For God's sake, stop!' The assistant manager with a pass key and the head porter answered the electrician's summons. The young woman who had been Heath's companion lay face-down and naked on the bed in the brightly lit room. Her buttocks and back were marked by the cane now in the hand of Neville Heath who was standing over her, also naked.

The rescue party were taken aback when the young woman refused to make a complaint against her assailant, let alone bring charges against him. She and Heath were told to leave the hotel. They did so, arm-in-arm, and went off together in a taxi. Was the young woman embarrassed at the publicity which proceedings against Heath might entail? Or was she what the 1940s called a 'slapperat', underworld slang for a masochist? She was later tracked down and interviewed by the police. In her statement she claimed that she had not been a willing party to the bedroom activities but declined to prosecute her companion. Detective Inspector Reg Spooner, later to investigate Margery Gardner's murder, reported that when questioned point-blank about her evasiveness, the young woman in the Strand Palace Hotel incident admitted that 'she had gone knowingly with Heath to the bedroom to be stripped and beaten.'

If Heath was indulging in such behaviour with young women over a period of several years, as he claimed, it seems remarkable that he never faced criminal charges. His explanation to Hill was that 'society girls are the best bet. They're used to hard riding, both with horses and men.' He professed to have no respect for educated middle-class girls, remarking that in any case, after such an incident, 'they're always too ashamed to make a fuss'.

There was a calculating plausibility in this. James Camb, a sexually overactive steward on the *Durban Castle* who was convicted of the murder at sea of the actress Gay Gibson in 1947, described a squabble in another girl's cabin on the previous voyage. 'She exasperated me by her teenage behaviour. I put her over my knee and gave her a good spanking.' A complaint from her would have meant his dismissal. But, like Heath's partners, she had already invited his sexual attentions. Rape would have been a serious matter and a subject for outrage. Something of the sort that Camb described, however, might simply have made the complainant look ridiculous, as a grown woman who had been treated like an ill-mannered child. Heath was probably right in attributing lack of 'fuss' to a fear of being greeted with general amusement.

In the months following the incident at the Strand Palace Hotel, he maintained the charade of 'Lieutenant Colonel Jimmy Armstrong, DFC and Africa Star' of the South African Air Force. Sometimes he reverted to his own name, but with nothing less than the rank of Lieutenant Colonel. On 5 April he was fined £10 at Wimbledon Magistrates Court for wearing a uniform and medal ribbons to which he was not entitled.

He lived in two worlds. One was the Fleet Street of bars

and clubs, the Cheshire Cheese, the Falstaff and the St Anne's Club, where he could rub shoulders with journalists. Heath was supposed to be studying for his Class B civilian pilot's licence. On the strength of this, he would be able to fly journalists anywhere in the world. A friend from his RAF days had offered him a job as test pilot with a light aircraft firm. He might combine the test flights and the Continental trips. But he did nothing whatever towards getting the job or his licence, apart from giving journalists the impression that he had already passed the necessary exams as a pilot. A number of them paid him money for flights that they would never make.

His other life was spent in the bohemia and underworld of Chelsea and Knightsbridge. He lived at the Normandie Hotel, dined and danced at the Panama Club, drank at the Trevor Arms or in the chic old-fashioned bar of the Nag's Head. Among his companions were the public-school burglars and the men and women of questionable sexual tastes. He was watched by the Ghost Squad, not as a sadist but as a burglar, his pre-war convictions being on record. Inspector John Capstick thought at one point that Heath might be the leader of the gang which specialized in opening the wall-safes of the wealthy in Chelsea and Knightsbridge. Heath and his companions were tailed wherever they went. On one occasion, Capstick followed them to a restaurant in Sloane Street, saw them order an expensive meal and retired to his car. As he sat down, he discovered that during his absence someone had coated the driver's seat thickly with treacle. The lid of the treacle tin was on the back seat, a lipsticked kiss impressed on it by one of the gang's women.

Such was the shadow-world of Neville Heath in the spring and early summer of 1946. As Spooner put the story together on the night following Margery Gardner's death, the pattern was plain. Heath was a trickster and a sadist. Looking back on his career, it was possible to see how every step had led him on the path to murder. Criminality and perversion were the driving forces of his conduct. Margery Gardner was the victim who had been attacked, overpowered, tied to the bed, thrashed and suffocated. But had it not happened to her, Heath's murderous instincts dictated that it would have happened to his next bedroom partner, perhaps, or the one after that.

4

It was in early May that Neville Heath's friend Peter Tilley-Bailey had introduced him to Margery Gardner at the Panama Club. That meeting marked the beginning of a mutually fatal relationship. Ironically, she was by no means the most important girl in Heath's life that summer. On 15 June, he met Yvonne S. at a dance in Chelsea. As if in a wartime romance, there was love within hours, rather than weeks or months. The following day they became engaged and she returned for the night to his room and his bed at the Pembridge Court Hotel, the very room and bed where Margery Gardner was to be found five days later. Never did Yvonne find him anything but gentle, considerate and affectionate.

By the time that Margery Gardner's body was found, Neville Heath had been gone for more than twelve hours. Packing his belongings into a suitcase, he went quietly down the stairs from the hotel bedroom, slipped past the front door and closed it after him. Carrying his case, he made his way through the quiet streets of Kensington and Belgravia to the Grosvenor Hotel, for an early breakfast. One entrance of the hotel was on the concourse of Victoria station. He caught an early train to Worthing, where Yvonne lived with her parents, and booked in at the Ocean Hotel.

He did not conceal the death of Margery Gardner from his fiancée. On that Saturday evening, 22 June, the day after the discovery of Margery Gardner's body, he took Yvonne to dinner at the Blue Peter Club at Angmering. During dinner, he confided to her how he had left the Pembridge Court Hotel on Thursday to stay with friends in north London and how Margery Gardner's body was found on Friday after a man known to Heath as 'Jack' had used the room. Heath had given all the help he could to the police.

Next day, however, the Sunday morning newspapers reported for the first time that the police were looking for Neville Heath. Yvonne telephoned him at the Ocean Hotel. Her parents had read the papers and were very concerned. 'Yes,' Heath said casually, 'I thought they would be.' He explained that the police merely wanted to go over certain details with him and that he had already telephoned

Superintendent Barratt. He was going up to London and would be back shortly. He left the Ocean Hotel and vanished.

That Sunday evening, Group Captain Rupert Brooke booked in at the Tollard Royal Hotel on Bournemouth's West Overcliff.

5

There was an air of the unreal and the bizarre about almost every aspect of the Neville Heath manhunt. To choose 'Group Captain Rupert Brooke' as an alias seemed absurd, as if he had chosen 'Wing Commander William Wordsworth' or something of the kind. But precisely because it would have been such an outlandish choice, it seemed almost convincing. He found not the least difficulty with it at the Tollard Royal Hotel. If Neville Heath was insane, as was soon to be argued, he demonstrated that a madman is in many respects more difficult to hunt than one who is sane.

Equally odd was the silence that Spooner encountered as his undercover officers filtered into the clubs and pubs which were the habitat of a criminal and sexual underworld in Chelsea, Kensington and Soho. The average criminal disapproved of murder, especially of sex murder, as strongly as the law-abiding. Perpetrators of sexual crime were the pariahs of the prison system. Why were Margery Gardner's associates and the other inhabitants of this twilight zone so downright unhelpful? News of this reached the press. After the manhunt had been in progress for twelve days without any result, the *Evening Standard* reported on 2 July that Scotland Yard was trying 'to break down a murder silence in Chelsea'. The report added that, 'In clubs, cafés and bars, studios and hotels – these two men are well known. They are Heath and a man named Laurie Kearns. Police want to interview both. The people who knew them well refuse to talk. Women friends of the two men deny knowledge of their moves just before the murder.'

Laurie Kearns was entirely innocent of any involvement. His name was only mentioned because a handkerchief with his laundry-mark had been found in the hotel bedroom. But the silence about Heath seemed inexplicable. He had been seen with Margery Gardner by a good number of people at the Trevor Arms in Knightsbridge and by even more at Peter Tilley-Bailey's party at the Panama Club in the hours before the young woman's death. Even Margery Gardner's friends were suddenly unwilling to say what they knew. It began to seem like a murder inquiry with more to be discovered than anyone had supposed. One of the police officers in the case later said privately and sombrely that Margery Gardner had been 'asking for it'. Asking for what? To be murdered? To be beaten in such a manner that it would have brought a prosecution from the RSPCA if it had been done to a horse? The suggestions seemed preposterous and, in any case, no person can consent in law to be murdered.

Heath was reported as having been seen all over the country and in Dublin. He was quite capable of getting abroad, perhaps to somewhere like Spain with no extradition treaty. Flying clubs as well as airports were closely watched. But the only response came from Heath himself. It was a letter postmarked 'Worthing' and dated 23 June, addressed to Superintendent Barratt at Scotland Yard. Heath explained how he had lent his hotel room to Margery Gardner and a friend of hers known to him only as 'Jack'. He had come back to the room at 3 a.m. and found her 'in the condition of which you are aware'. He had been reluctant to come forward and help because it would mean he must also 'face the music of a fraud charge' for which he was wanted. He had therefore packed his belongings and left. If the police wished to reply to him, they should do so through the personal column of the *Daily Telegraph*.

The letter seemed mad, whether or not its author was. His alibi was no alibi at all, since plenty of people had seen him with Margery Gardner just before her death. There was also something surreal about conducting a murder investigation through the personal column of the *Daily Telegraph*. Neville Heath, if ever he had had contact with reality, had surely lost it now.

The police investigation got no further as the fortnight passed. In Bournemouth, Group Captain Rupert Brooke with his pipe and his easy-going democratic manners, his stories of narrow escapes and comic incidents on active service, charmed the guests of the Tollard Royal Hotel. He explained that he was only in Bournemouth until an Auster light aircraft at Hurn airport was ready for delivery to the

Continent. Before long, he was due back in South Africa, where he had entered himself for the 1947 King's Cup Air Race. No one who heard him doubted a single word.

He seemed a generous young fellow, standing drinks at the hotel bar, asking the barman to put the cost down on his 'crime-sheet'. He also had plans to roll back the hotel lounge carpet, put some big band swing on the radiogram, and organize dances. He had made a girlfriend or two on the promenades of the Undercliff and this surprised no one. On Wednesday 3 July, he came back to tea with an attractive brunette of nineteen, Doreen Marshall, who had been demobbed from the WRENS the previous month. She had measles before that and had come to Bournemouth for a holiday. The couple were getting on extremely well and it seemed predictable that Group Captain Brooke should invite Miss Marshall to have dinner with him at the hotel that evening. She went back to the Norfolk Hotel, where she was staying, to change.

Dinner was quite a success, though Doreen Marshall appeared rather tired afterwards and anxious to go back to her hotel. At about 11 p.m., at her request, one of the other guests asked the night porter to get her a taxi. Shortly after this, Group Captain Brooke told the porter to cancel the taxi. He and Miss Marshall would walk the half mile or so to the Norfolk Hotel. As they set off and rain clouds filled the sky of the summer night, Heath promised the porter that he would be back in half an hour. Doreen Marshall turned and said, 'He'll be back in quarter of an hour.' Group Captain Brooke was not seen again for five hours, and Doreen Marshall was never seen alive again.

By 4 a.m. Group Captain Brooke had still not arrived back at the hotel entrance. The night porter peeped into his room and was puzzled to find him in bed and asleep. Next morning, the affable young officer teased the porter, saying that he had decided to come in via a builder's ladder at the rear of the premises. The joke seemed to be in character.

Three days later, Doreen Marshall's disappearance from the Norfolk Hotel became the subject of a police inquiry. Mr Relf, the manager of the Tollard Royal, suggested to Group Captain Brooke that he ought to go to Bournemouth police station and give what information he could, since he might well have been the last person to see the missing girl. The young officer agreed at once, saying that he understood Doreen Marshall had been going off to Exeter for a few days with an American officer, Pat Wisecarver, to whom she was unofficially engaged.

On the evening of Saturday 6 July, he went to the police station in Madeira Road and was interviewed by PC Souter. He explained that he had walked back with Doreen Marshall as far as the Central Gardens by the pier. She then said that she could easily walk back alone to the Norfolk Hotel, which was just across The Square at the centre of Bournemouth and up Richmond Hill. He was most concerned to hear now that she was missing. Though he could not swear to having seen her after the night of 3 July, he thought he glimpsed her going into Bobby's department store in Old Christchurch Road the next morning. After that, he supposed she had gone to Exeter with her American friend.

All this seemed entirely genuine. The police had done their duty, knowing that when a respectable girl went missing the odds were still massively in favour of her having gone off with a man and against her having been murdered or harmed. The visitor made his statement and signed it. Then Souter led him out into the police station vestibule and Group Captain Brooke was almost on his way again. At that moment a middle-aged man and a young woman came in from Madeira Road and walked towards Souter. Group Captain Brooke's face went white and he trembled badly enough for Souter to see it. His hand went up to his neck, round which he wore an RAF aircrew 'escape scarf' with a map of Germany printed on it. As he pulled it loose, there were scratches on his neck. The young woman was Mrs Cruikshank. She was Doreen Marshall's elder sister but as like her as a twin. Group Captain Brooke looked as if he had seen a ghost.

He did not leave the police station. The incident in the vestibule recalled to PC Souter's mind a photograph in the *Police Gazette*. He led the suspect back to the interview room, sat him down, and said, 'Isn't your name Heath?' Group Captain Brooke thought that rather a joke. Of course his name was not Heath. But he admitted that a few people had said to him that he looked like the wanted man. It was a natural mistake on Souter's part. Unfortunately for the suspect, no photographs of Heath had appeared in the press, other than in the *Police Gazette*. Therefore the only person likely to think that Brooke looked like Heath was Heath himself.

His belongings were fetched from the Tollard Royal Hotel, including a cloakroom ticket for Bournemouth West railway station. This produced a suitcase. It contained a hat and mackintosh, a blue woollen scarf, and a diamond-weave whip. At 9.45 p.m., Group Captain Brooke was told that he would be detained as Neville George Clevely Heath, pending the arrival of officers from Scotland Yard. He would then be interviewed 'in connection with the murder of Margery Gardner in London on 20 or 21 June this year'. Heath seemed not to mind. 'Oh, all right,' he said.

Two days later, after police had combed the wooded chines on the coast between Bournemouth and Poole without success, the naked body of Doreen Marshall was found by a girl walking her dog in Branksome Dene Chine. She had been murdered, but not as Margery Gardner had been murdered. The details of Margery Gardner's murder suggested planning and cold calculation: the undressing, the positioning on the bed, the tying down and the gagging. It was almost ritualistic. In Doreen Marshall's case, she had been the victim of a horrific attack by a maniac with a knife.

So far as the methods of the two murders were concerned, they might almost have been committed by two different types, let alone two different men: the suave bedroom sadist and the ripper of the dark streets. They were, however, one man's work, though Neville Heath was never tried for Doreen Marshall's murder. In the two days before his arrest, he sold to a Bournemouth jeweller a fob-watch belonging to the young WREN and also pawned a diamond ring that had been hers. In his jacket pocket Souter found the return half of a first-class ticket from Waterloo to Bournemouth. Its number and the records of the Regent Street travel agency confirmed that it was Doreen Marshall's.

There was a curiosity about the second death, though it did not exonerate Heath. Doreen Marshall had insisted that she was going straight back to the Norfolk Hotel after dinner at the Tollard Royal. But she was murdered a mile away in the opposite direction. How or why she went there, apparently against her will on a well-frequented seaside promenade, was never to be explained.

6

Because English law allows a man to be tried for only one murder at a time, Neville Heath was tried for the murder of Margery Gardner and was never convicted of any crime against Doreen Marshall. However, the plea of insanity, offered in the Margery Gardner case, seemed still more relevant in that of Doreen Marshall. The amiable Group Captain Brooke – who had also been the likeable Captain Jimmy Armstrong, a popular fund-raiser for charity with the Alexandra Rams in 1944 – bore no apparent resemblance to the maniac with the knife who had butchered his young victim in Branksome Dene Chine. As the killer of Doreen Marshall, would the jury not be more inclined to regard him as a lunatic? Faced with the horror of Branksome Dene Chine and the cheery young 'Group Captain', could anyone believe him sane? 'Mad as a hatter,' was the medical opinion given to Heath's defence counsel, J.D. 'Josh' Casswell, KC. But would a court – and a jury – believe it?

Theobald Mathew, Director of Public Prosecutions, studied the evidence and chose to play safe. He decided that Heath was to be tried for the murder of Margery Gardner. It would be easier, in that first case, to make a jury believe he was bad rather than mad. Branksome Dene Chine was to all appearances the work of a man who was utterly deranged rather than of sexual desire, however deviant. The evidence of Room 4 at the Pembridge Court Hotel did not necessarily indicate insanity. A young woman had been made to undress and lie on the bed. She had been tied down, gagged, whipped and suffocated. A taste for perversion, an assault upon innocence, a pillow over her face to silence her were the stuff of sex-murder as juries recognized it. Neville Heath might slip through the net and find sanctuary in Broadmoor on the Doreen Marshall evidence alone. Margery Gardner, if anyone, would lead him to the gallows.

After his death, it was said that the police suspected him of two earlier murders, one of a young WAAF near RAF Finmere in 1944 and one of a prostitute near Victoria station, both showing a madman's violence. There was never any proof and, of course, no allusion to the suspicions at his trial.

Could Neville Heath be shown to be insane? If so, it would

save his life.

On the basis of the so-called M'Naghten Rules of 1843, it might not be easy to build a defence of insanity for Heath in the Margery Gardner case. There seemed little doubt he was mad in other terms. Under the rules, it would be necessary for Casswell to show that either his client had not known what he was doing when he murdered Margery Gardner or that he did not know that what he was doing was wrong. It was established that before Heath met Margery Gardner at the Trevor Arms, he had downed twenty-four pints of beer since lunchtime. The taxi-driver recalled that as the couple went up the hotel steps, the amount they had drunk made it necessary for them to support each other. Drunkenness is not insanity. However, the trial judge in Heath's case was the future Lord Morris of Borth-y-Gest. 'Drunkenness can never be an excuse for crime,' he had recently said in another case, but he qualified this by adding, 'There may be drunkenness of so extreme a form that a drunken man may be wholly incapable of forming the intent to commit the crime.'

The difficulty for the defence was that it might be relatively easy to show that Heath, in his staggering intoxication, did not appreciate the extent of each sadistic detail in his treatment of Margery Gardner. Certainly his inhibitions would have been weakened. However, no jury was likely to believe that he overpowered her, stripped her, tied her to the bed and gagged her without knowing it.

When Casswell interviewed Heath in Brixton prison, his heart sank. Heath was debonair and well-groomed. He looked 'the exact opposite' of a juror's idea of a madman. Heath cheerfully announced that he was going to plead guilty. His counsel was completely taken aback by this and suggested that, for the sake of his family alone, he should offer some defence of his actions. 'All right,' said Heath amiably. 'Put me down as not guilty, old boy.'

There was, to say the least, something zany about his attitude to the trial. His letters to his friends referred breezily to the prison governor as 'The boss', and Brixton prison as 'The old firm'. Heath was to be presented to the court as a 'moral defective'. The nature of the defence made it virtually impossible to send him into the witness-box. He would not sound like a lunatic nor a moral defective, but a plausibly decent and intelligent young fellow. This psychopathic duality was the key to his personality, but Casswell dared not risk Heath turning his charm on the jurors. Therefore, the only defence witnesses would be those called to show that Heath was deranged.

Casswell's star witness was a major authority in the world of psychiatric medicine, his speciality being criminal psychology. He had not the least doubt of Heath's insanity or his own ability to convince a jury of this. Dr William Henry de Bargue Hubert was in his forties. He had been psychotherapist at Wormwood Scrubs for five years until 1939 and then psychiatric adviser to Middle East Command. At the end of the war he became psychotherapist at Feltham prison and Broadmoor. As joint author of the standard text-book on the subject, *The Psychological Treatment of Crime*, he had examined Heath and pronounced him insane within the meaning of the M'Naghten Rules.

'In my opinion, this man ought to have been classified when young as a mental defective,' Dr Hubert concluded. 'He did not know he was doing wrong at the time of the murders.' Specifically, he argued, the defendant was a moral defective. If Dr Hubert could demonstrate that in court, Neville Heath might be spared. Moreover Dr Hubert was the big name of the trial. Though the Crown had two witnesses to rebut him, Dr Hubert Young and Dr Henry Grierson, they were merely prison medical officers from Brixton and Wormwood Scrubs with no specialist knowledge or experience of psychiatry. It seemed that Dr Hubert might have a clear run.

When the trial began, Anthony Hawke KC, for the Crown, outlined the events of 20–21 June 1946. He called witnesses to prove them, though he was careful not to refer to the murder of Doreen Marshall or any other crimes alleged against Heath. If Heath could be shown to be insane, the extent of his crimes might count for nothing. Indeed, the more horrific they seemed, the more insane he might appear.

Casswell's star witness was to give evidence on the second day of the trial. Dr Hubert was now well-briefed with proven instances of Heath's bedroom sadism, at the Strand Palace Hotel, the Normandie Hotel, and elsewhere. Heath's conduct seemed that of a long-term moral defective, but it also suggested that there had been no intent to kill Margery Gardner. Unlike the previous occasions, it might be argued that this was a bedroom melodrama that had gone horrifically wrong. The fate of the moral defective was to be a partner in that grotesque and fatal misadventure.

But was not Neville Heath still the dark phantom who had launched himself upon an unsuspecting young woman? She was certainly not unsuspecting. Hubert's information confirmed that Heath's partner at the Normandie Hotel scandal in May had been Margery Gardner. The hotel had urged her to prosecute the man who had whipped her. According to Heath's former adjutant, Paull Hill, a dismayed Margery Gardner hastily explained that she dared not risk the notoriety as her husband was a senior army officer serving abroad. In fact, her husband Peter Gardner was a wine salesman in Sheffield.

If all this could be put before the jury, might it not be shown that Heath, standing at one side of the bed, bringing down the whip with his right hand, could have pushed the young woman's head down with his left? In the previous twelve hours, he had consumed twenty-four pints of beer in central London, four more at the Trevor Arms, and an unspecified amount of drink at the Panama Club. Might he not have put his left hand down to hold Margery Gardner still, too fuddled to realize that it required only the obstruction of her nostrils to kill her?

Misadventure did not invalidate the argument of moral insanity. Moral insanity was there in Heath all the time, said Dr Hubert. It was the misadventure with Margery Gardner which brought it to the notice of the law. It was not to be expected that the jury would acquit Heath. However, they might find him insane, or judge that he was guilty of manslaughter. If he was guilty of murder, they or the Home Secretary might find grounds for recommending mercy. They were concerned with Margery Gardner's death alone. In that respect, Heath's crime recalled another ex-officer and gentleman, Ronald True, who had been sentenced to death for the murder of Olive Young after the First World War and who had been reprieved on the grounds of his insanity.

All this depended on Dr Hubert. There was some disquiet when he failed to appear at the Old Bailey. Then, at last, the only man who might save Heath's life arrived. Dr Hubert was late and in a state of extreme nervous agitation. He said something about his taxi being involved in a collision but

Casswell guessed there was worse than that. He now discovered that his star witness, for all his medical fame, was a hopeless drug addict. Indeed, Hubert committed suicide by means of an overdose in the following year. The hurry and the collision had deprived him of his chance to administer his morning stimulant.

Casswell had already told the jury that his defence was to show Heath's insanity. For that, he relied on Dr Hubert, who was now in a state of nervous anguish. There was no one else and the court was waiting. Casswell took his place. Presently Dr Hubert was called. He appeared, a changed man with the aid of self-administered narcotics. He was confident, happy and floating on a cloud of drug-induced euphoria. Whatever he said sounded to him telling and clever. In examination, he told Casswell that Heath suffered from a deficient moral sense – moral insanity. 'At times he is unaware that what he is doing is wrong.'

This was the way Casswell understood that Hubert would argue the case, though Heath's moral deficiency was supposed to be permanent. Hubert went on to describe how Heath was quite lucid most of the time, then a darkness would come upon him and he would commit a crime, afterwards returning to apparent normality. Murder committed in this way was a common theme of film melodrama at the time and something the jury would recognize. Unfortunately, Hubert then went on to say that it applied to all Heath's crimes. Darkness would come over him and he would embezzle mess funds, write cheques that bounced, borrow money without repaying it. The theory, so convincing to Dr Hubert in the realms of euphoria, began to sound like an intellectual trick in the Old Bailey courtroom. Casswell struggled on. When Heath emerged from these dark moods of madness, he would presumably appreciate that he had done wrong? 'Other people might,' said Dr Hubert airily, 'but I think basically he does not regard it as wrong.'

This assertion that Heath never regarded his acts as wrong flatly contradicted what Hubert had said a few minutes earlier, that Heath was only unaware of the wrong 'at times'. The jurors stared at the prisoner impassively. They had by now listened to the defence account of how Doreen Marshall had been butchered, her young life cut short in the most atrocious way. The handsome well-groomed figure in the dock was a man intelligent enough to have flown a bomber on active service. Did he even now, after hearing the recital of the atrocity, not think that what he had done was wrong? That was what Dr Hubert was telling them. They looked at Heath and knew the Hubert theory was rubbish.

It seemed that Hubert had abandoned – or forgotten – the carefully prepared defence and was just making up answers as he went along. He contradicted himself, even under Casswell's questioning. Casswell called the performance 'absolutely appalling'. The first rule of examination is not to ask questions to which one does not know the answers. It was impossible to know what Hubert might say next. The only course was to cut short the questions and sit down before Hubert did any more damage. As Casswell sat down, a note in Heath's handwriting was passed from the dock. 'This evidence is Hubert's opinion – not what I have suggested he say on my behalf.'

Anthony Hawke got up, courteous, cool, precise and deadly. There followed a ritual slaughter of Hubert's evidence. When it was over, however, Dr Hubert was on top of the world. He confided to Casswell how pleased he was to have tied Anthony Hawke in knots. He began by assuring Hawke that Heath would not have known that what he did to Margery Gardner was wrong. Given Heath's sexual compulsions and his drunkenness, perhaps that might be proved. Instead, Hubert soon disproved it, as Hawke asked.

'When he suffocated that woman, having lashed her, tied her up and made her helpless first, he knew it was wrong?'

'No,' said Hubert firmly.

'Would you tell me why?'

'Because people during sexual behaviour generally consider what they are doing is right and their own business.'

Casswell, looking on in dismay, described Dr Hubert's answers as 'quite ghastly'. He was now, apparently, saying that any perpetrator of a sex crime was exempt from legal proceedings on the grounds of insanity.

'Then may I take it this is your evidence. At the time he was inflicting these injuries, he thought it was right?'

'He thought it was ...' Hubert stopped, caught between having to say 'yes', which would sound preposterous, or 'no', which would contradict his entire argument.

'Yes,' he said confidently. 'He thought it was right.'

'He thought it was right?'

'Yes.'

Worse still, Hawke cross-examined Hubert on the question of Heath's sadism. Hubert said that because it was a means of obtaining sexual satisfaction, Heath must have thought sadism right.

'Would it be your view that a person who finds it convenient at the moment to forge a cheque is entitled to claim exemption from the responsibility on the grounds of insanity?'

'Yes.'

It was a truly dreadful performance, all the worse because Hubert thought he was doing it superbly well. There was worse to come. If Heath were a sadist, Hawke asked, were there cases of this in his past history. There were, Hubert assured him.

'Similar acts without such consequences have occurred before,' he explained.

'When?'

'At different dates in the past.'

'Could you give them me?'

The defence waited to hear of the Strand Palace Hotel, the Normandie …

'Could you give them me?' Hawke asked quietly.

'No,' said Dr Hubert. He had known them once but now they had floated from him.

And still there was worse to come. Hubert insisted that Heath's ultimate defence was that he was a moral defective. Of that there could be no doubt.

'I want to understand that,' Hawke said. 'Are you saying that this man is in law a moral defective?'

'Yes,' said Hubert, suddenly and fatally becoming an authority on law as well as psychiatry.

Hawke read out the relevant clause of the Mental Deficiency Act of 1927, which stipulated that a man who is a moral or mental defective must be so classified before the age of eighteen. Heath had never been examined, let alone classified.

'He cannot possibly be a moral defective, can he?' Hawke asked.

'It is difficult to prove,' said Dr Hubert vaguely.

The destruction of the defence case by Dr Hubert meant that far from Heath's insanity being debated and disproved, it was never even discussed in any worthwhile manner.

7

There was one other issue in the case. Did Heath intend to kill Margery Gardner? No one entering Room 4 at the Pembridge Court Hotel on 21 June doubted it for an instant. It was the most lurid, perverted, sadistic murder of the age. Or was it? If it could be shown that he did not intend it, there was not an automatic defence but it might save his life.

As Anthony Hawke suggested it, Neville Heath had lured Margery Gardner to his hotel room. There he had threatened her or by other means made her undress, perhaps stripped her himself. He had thrown her or forced her face-down on the bed and tied her hands and feet. Then he had gagged her. After that, he had thrashed her with a riding whip. Finally he had forced a pillow over her face and suffocated her, presumably to prevent her telling the story of her ordeal. At the widest latitude, this happened between midnight and 2 a.m.

That was the story as the court, the press and the public heard it. But common sense alone prompted one persistent doubt about its accuracy.

There were several rooms on each floor of the hotel. Heath's was at the front of the building, looking out across the gardens of Pembridge Square. The hotel was almost fully booked. Other guests were sleeping in rooms either side and above. Whatever Heath did, he did it in a silent hotel, in the middle of the night, with a dozen people sleeping within twenty feet, beyond walls or ceiling. Not one of them heard a sound.

If he lured Margery Gardner to the hotel, did she not struggle, cry out, protest or even argue when at last he threatened her? Heath was strongly built but even so to accomplish such an assault in total silence would have been impossible. Moreover, Margery Gardner was not a casual pick-up but a young woman who had been a friend of his for some weeks and whom he described as 'a good little scout'.

Thanks to Dr Hubert's euphoria, there was a factor in this

which was not brought out in evidence. It was first publicly referred to in a comment on Margery Gardner in the *News of the World* on 29 September 1946, after Heath was condemned to death. 'She knew she was dealing with an abnormal man when she went to the hotel in which she died. She must have known she would be thrashed and she was certainly aware of the riding switch and its purpose.'

Such was the first hint of a story the court and the public had never heard. Fragments of a puzzle – the refusal of her friends to talk to the police or the apparently preposterous comment of the police officer who muttered that she had been 'asking' for trouble – began to take their place in the design. The *News of the World* then revealed that Margery Gardner and Neville Heath had been thrown out of a hotel – the Normandie in Knightsbridge – some weeks earlier, after Margery Gardner's cries had been heard during another bedroom drama.

Was it merely a piece of sensational journalism? Apparently not. That the young woman was a masochist was first confirmed by Dr Keith Simpson, who found on Margery Gardner's body not only the marks made at the Pembridge Court Hotel but traces of an earlier encounter, perhaps that with Heath at the Normandie. Inspector Reg Spooner also confirmed her tastes from his knowledge of Margery Gardner. She not merely permitted such treatment by her lovers 'but encouraged it'. From the documents passed to the defence, Casswell knew of the incident involving Heath and the blonde at the Strand Palace Hotel in February and also that at the Normandie in May. He later wrote that Margery Gardner had been 'heavily thrashed' by Heath in May because evidence of this was still visible when Keith Simpson examined her on 21 June.

When seen in this light, the case against Heath was altered again. That he killed Margery Gardner was not in doubt. That he intended to kill her became not only uncertain but doubtful. He had signed the hotel register with his own name. That name had been known to the police since 1937. If a young woman was found dead in his room, he would be the only suspect. The entire clientele of the Panama Club had just seen him with Margery Gardner, so had the doorman and the taxi driver. The last thing he would willingly or sensibly do would be to commit murder in that place at that time.

Thanks to Dr Hubert, Casswell faced a procedural problem

in dealing with this. He later wrote that he was convinced that Heath was a sadist but equally convinced that he did not premeditate murder either with Margery Gardner or Doreen Marshall. What had happened at the Pembridge Court Hotel? It seems that Margery Gardner knew about the whip before she left the Panama Club, that she mentioned it to friends and also told them that she was going to spend the night with Heath. If she did not say that he was going to use it, at least she left that conclusion in their minds.

Casswell could not introduce evidence for himself, telling the jurors a story which had not been presented by witnesses. The fact that Margery Gardner was a masochist was known to a good many of those at the trial, but not to the jury. The fact that on at least two occasions that year Heath had been found with women who were consenting partners in his acts was also known to a good many people in court, but not to the jurors. There were cryptic references during the trial to 'the Strand Palace Hotel', to 'the incident in the London hotel', and to 'a certain case not mentioned here'. That was as close as the jurors were allowed to get, and they seemed a little puzzled.

On 13 July, Heath had completed an account of his sexual history for his defence lawyers. There was also a document headed 'Confidential and Medical', drawn up for the Crown. Between them, these substantiated Casswell's belief that Heath had a record of sado-masochistic encounters with women who were consenting partners, as well as with those who were not. To establish that Heath and Margery Gardner had gone to the Pembridge Court Hotel with an agreed purpose of this kind might save the prisoner from the gallows. Ironically for Heath, the witness who could have saved him was the young woman whom he had killed. Late in the trial, when Casswell was cross-examining the Crown's rebuttal witnesses, he tried to introduce the two documents.

Dr Hugh Grierson, Senior Medical Officer at Brixton Prison, was one of Hawke's rebuttal witnesses in respect of Dr Hubert's theories of insanity. Casswell produced the document headed 'Confidential and Medical'. He handed it to Dr Grierson, in the hope of discussing its contents. But Dr Grierson said that he had never seen it before and handed it back.

Last of all, Casswell handed Grierson a copy of Heath's

own account of his sexual history, dated 13 July. Grierson said that he had not seen that either and handed it back. At this point, Mr Justice Morris intervened, saying to Casswell, 'I assume you are not making these exhibits but just asking the witness to look at them?' As politely as possible, he was warning Casswell that the contents of the documents could not be introduced in evidence now that the defence case was closed.

With the exclusion of those documents, Heath was doomed. On 26 September 1946, it took the jury just an hour to find him guilty, with no question of insanity and no recommendation to mercy. He was sentenced to death.

Heath refused to appeal, adamant that he would rather be hanged than sent to Broadmoor. There was no reprieve and he was executed on 26 October at Pentonville. As the partition of the death cell was folded back and the gallows-trap was revealed with its beam and coiled rope, a tot of whisky was poured for him. According to Albert Pierrepoint the hangman, Neville Heath, debonair in grey pin-stripe suit, spoke his last words to the warder with the bottle. 'I say, old man, you might make that a double.'

'Mad as a hatter', had been the psychiatric view given to Casswell. But that defence had crumbled in court with Dr Hubert's blithe assurance that a man who forged a cheque was entitled to be acquitted as insane if he felt his forgery was the right thing to do. With the collapse of Hubert went all hope of establishing Heath's insanity. Yet it need not have happened. Hubert was the authority in the case. The rebuttal witnesses were two non-specialist medical officers from London prisons.

With Hubert too went the chance of establishing that Heath and Margery Gardner had only set out to do what they had done before, when both were sober rather than drunk. This would have meant explaining to the jury that the young woman was a masochist; that she apparently allowed, even suggested, the use of the gag in the quietness of the hotel at night. Would a jury believe it? Would it seem credible that any woman would permit – let alone want – Heath to tie her down and inflict such marks with the riding-whip? Casswell might have quoted Havelock Ellis's account of 'Florrie' and other literature on the subject. More to the point, the other evidence was surely consistent only with Margery Gardner being a partner at the outset rather than a dupe or a victim.

Had the whole truth been told, would it have saved Neville Heath from the gallows in this case?

8

Had Dr Hubert been in a state to testify intelligently and with proper documentation, the defence of insanity would have been much strengthened. It might also have opened the way to a complete account of the circumstances of Margery Gardner's death, suggesting the element of misadventure or accident. That Heath caused her death was not denied. That he intended to cause it was certainly not credible. But neither masochism nor drunkenness was properly revealed in the course of the trial. That Heath had indulged in sado-masochism with other partners was not mentioned. Whatever the verdict, however unappealing the character of Neville Heath and however abhorrent his crimes, he went to the gallows for a crime he surely never intended and one which, as murder, perhaps he did not commit.

In general, the law required that a man should have the intention, the *mens rea*, to commit the crime. But it also presumed that a man was responsible for the natural and probable outcome of his acts. Even if he did not intend to commit murder, he was guilty of murder if it occurred as the result of another crime, in this case grievous bodily harm.

In one important respect, the law was confused. Grievous bodily harm had, apparently, occurred twice between Heath and young women that year with the consent of both parties on each occasion. No one can consent to be murdered but, plainly, a person may consent to be injured in a boxing match under the Queensberry Rules to an extent which would otherwise be grievous bodily harm. What happened where the consent related to sexual gratification?

The law was confused and remained so until 1992, when a majority of the House of Lords decided that sado-masochistic acts between consenting partners did not enjoy the exemption which the law gave to boxing or rugby. It was therefore criminal. In 1946, however, the leading case was *R v. Donovan* (1934). In that case a man had caned a woman for their mutual sexual gratification and had been prosecuted.

He was convicted but the conviction was quashed on appeal. It was certainly within the law to punish children and, until 1948, courts imposed sentences of flogging quite as severe as the beating of Margery Gardner.

There had also been other cases in which sexual practices had led to the death of one of the partners. In one of these, at the end of the war, a serviceman had been charged with the murder of his girlfriend. The cause of her death was not immediately established. It was then proved that he had, allegedly at her suggestion, blown air into her vagina as a means of exciting her. This formed an embolism, of which she died. Though he was responsible for her death, he was acquitted of murder.

Even with all the evidence, Heath would have been convicted of manslaughter at the least and very probably murder. But, apart from the issue of his sanity, two sets of mitigating circumstances might have been established. The first would have suggested that what was presented as an unexpected attack or assault upon Margery Gardner was, in truth, a bedroom melodrama that went tragically wrong. The second related to his drunkenness.

Neville Heath had been dead for eleven years before such fatalities as the death of Margery Gardner were considered to be something other than capital murder, in the category of 'diminished responsibility' provided by the Homicide Act of 1957. Elsewhere, one of the most fully documented cases was the manslaughter of Mary Hennessee at Kansas City, Missouri, in 1985. Like Margery Gardner, she engaged in masochistic practices and played that role with other men and women. On the occasion which caused her death, a number of people were involved and the events continued for the greater part of the night. At intervals during what was later called an orgy, the young woman was severely beaten about the buttocks and thighs, far more so than Heath's partner. Apart from the ill-treatment to which she consented, she appeared to have suffered no other injury.

Two days later, the events of that night seemed to be no worse in their after effects than other occasions of that kind. Apart from considerable bruising and abrasions where she had been beaten, there was apparently no harm done. On the second day, however, Mary Hennessee developed breathing difficulties without warning, collapsed and died. She had been a reasonably healthy young woman and her sudden death was puzzling. When her body was examined, the marks of the beating were found but it was plain that they had not been received at the time of her death. Her partner in the orgy, as it was now called, later received a life sentence for her manslaughter. The cause of death was the disintegration of fatty tissue under the blows of the whip across her buttocks. 'Fatty emboli', microscopic globules of fat, had eventually broken away and entered the blood stream. The young woman had no reason to think she required hospital treatment or that her injuries were more than appeared as a result of her lover's attentions. But the entry of fatty emboli into the blood stream leads to their deposit in the heart, lungs, or other vital organs. In Mary Hennessee's case, the emboli reached the lungs. Unable to breath, she collapsed and died.

One of the most detailed cases concerned the death of Patricia Horby on 14 October 1987. It occurred in a remote house near the top of the Bussang Pass, in the hills of the Vosges. Patricia Horby was described by the police as an attractive young woman with short-cut hair, twenty-seven years old with two children. She was found tied naked and face-down on a bed in circumstances similar to Margery Gardner. Forensic examination established that intercourse had taken place not long before she died. The letter 'H' had been marked on the inner surface of each thigh, 'quite some time ago', in the view of the pathologist. A dog leash with which she had been strangled was still round her neck when her body was discovered.

Her husband, Jean Horby, admitted having strangled the young woman with the dog-leash. The issue for the police was whether or not he had done this because Patricia Horby had announced she was leaving him for another man, a commercial traveller whom she had met. Jealous anger might suggest mitigating circumstances, the distraught young man attacking his wife on hearing of her betrayal of their marriage. However, by the time of the trial the verdict turned on the issue of whether, after all, the strangling of Patricia Horby had not been a final and ungovernable expression of sadistic passion. Jean-Pierre Sentinelle, the pathologist, described some of the marks on Patricia Horby as dating from a previous beating. Combined with the discovery of her body tied to the bed, this suggested a calculated murder rather than a moment of jealous rage at her infidelity.

The husband revised his defence and now alleged that Patricia Horby was a masochist, a taste which he did not share. She had taunted him by the announcement of the new lover with whom she was going to live and whom she claimed had already beaten her. Jean Horby insisted that he only played the role of a sadist with reluctance and at the young woman's insistence. The evidence suggested that he had played it all the same over a considerable period of time. Patricia Horby's thirteen-year-old step-daughter had witnessed some of the young woman's ordeals and was able to identify other participants from photographs of the events which the couple kept. Patricia Horby's lesbian lover was traced and testified that both women were masochists who had encouraged Jean Horby and another man to behave towards them sadistically. In this account, Patricia Horby was the instigator rather than the victim of the things that were done to her. The lesbian lover of the dead woman displayed to the court a brand mark identical to that found on Patricia Horby and said that both recipients had been 'pleased' that the marks were made.

In June 1988, Jean Horby was convicted of intentional homicide. He had intended to use the leash, though he insisted that the strangling of his wife was a miscalculation. The court accepted that Patricia Horby was in part the instigator of the events which led to her death. The sentence on Jean Horby was therefore a mere four years' imprisonment.

Such insights into the complexities of sexual conduct, like the abolition of capital punishment itself, came far too late to save Neville Heath. The murder of Doreen Marshall was not a crime for which he stood trial. Had he done so, the grounds for regarding him as insane might have seemed much stronger. In the case of Margery Gardner, his fate was determined by the rules of evidence and the freak of misfortune which gave him a suicidal drug-addict as his expert witness. Heath was a likeable man to some who knew him but, at close quarters, an unattractive character. He was generally thought to have deserved his fate. In the light of what was not said at his trial, however, he seems far more like Ronald True, a candidate for a reprieve and a transfer to

Broadmoor. That he was so evidently a liar and a trickster, and the killer as well of Doreen Marshall, destroyed all public sympathy for him. Yet that second murder could have confirmed rather than disproved his madness.

There are cases in which 'hanged in error' is an assertion, an innocent man despatched on the gallows. In Heath's case, the words carry a question mark. It was, perhaps, his misfortune that in 1946 the question was not even asked. But that, of course, was as he wished. Repeatedly, he assured his parents and his friends that he would rather go to the gallows than live in a criminal lunatic asylum in the company of men like Ronald True.

5   The Shadow of a Gunman (1947)

1

The Prime Minister's son, writing to a friend in Italy about the post-war crime-wave, remarked sadly that there was 'little news from England but of robberies'. The crimes were perpetrated largely by soldiers who had been demobilized and the effect was that 'people are almost afraid of stirring after it is dark'. There had been an armed robbery in Piccadilly where members of the public had tried to intervene and had been driven off by the robbers. Small wonder that the shopkeepers and citizens of the capital lived in fear of the armed thug.

During the incidence of armed robbery in 1946–7 it might have been little consolation to know that the depressing letter was actually written almost two hundred years earlier, in 1750, by Horace Walpole to Sir Thomas Mann, after the peace of Aix-la-Chapelle in 1748 had concluded the War of the Austrian Succession.

The early months of 1947 brought additional miseries. They were the coldest and most uncomfortable in living memory. After Christmas the landscape was white with ice. Power shortages followed. The government, beset by post-war economic crises, rationed fuel and ordered the closing of cinemas during working hours to ease the demand on the electricity generating stations. Extra layers of clothing, all of it 'Utility', were obtainable only with coupons. Bread was now rationed and state-run 'British Restaurants' offered soup-kitchen fare. Never was it plainer that Hitler's war had brought Britain to the verge of bankruptcy than during that cold New Year. There was an Australian satirical song, 'Bankrupt Britannia', sung to the tune of 'Waltzing Matilda',

about British inability to pay war debts. The Labour government of Clement Attlee put out a pamphlet nationwide, *Battle
Together for Britain*, with such headings as 'All pull together
and we'll pull the country through.' Once again, the 'Dunkirk
Spirit' was invoked.

But there was a group in society whose ears were deaf to this
and its pockets a little fuller. Black marketeers, the 'spivs' and
'drones' of newspaper cartoons with snappy trilby hats, sharp
suits and padded shoulders, were the comically acceptable
face of a new underworld. Its other image was the culture of
the gun. Firearms, almost unknown in pre-war robbery, were
everywhere. There were Lugers taken by the hundred from
the defeated Wehrmacht as souvenirs in 1945–6. Small arms
'liberated' from the British or American armies were common,
the Bulldog Special revolver or the Webley .455. Some of the
weapons, like the Eley .455 of the later Craig and Bentley case,
predated the recent war. Some of the ammunition fired in
London streets in 1947 was more than fifty years old,
according to the firearms expert Robert Churchill. A good
many of the rounds failed to go off but those that did were no
less lethal because of their age.

As for the availability of guns, the older ones could be
bought as 'antiques' in second-hand shops. Folding shotguns
were obtainable without difficulty. They were not commonly
used by criminals because it was so easy to get hand-guns.
Even in 1952, Christopher Craig had owned forty guns of one
sort or another by the time he was sixteen. They were
swapped in the school playground. When the Commissioner
of Metropolitan Police, Sir Harold Scott, allowed an amnesty
for illegal weapons surrendered, 30,000 guns were handed in.
Others were retained by those who had a purpose for them.

The problem was compounded by the mass-circulation
press, never slow to sense a good story and to magnify an
individual crime into a national crisis. In November 1952, the
Daily Mail headlined: CHICAGO GUN-BATTLE IN
LONDON – GANGSTERS WITH MACHINE-GUN ON
ROOF KILL DETECTIVE, WOUND ANOTHER. The cas-
ualties had occurred but the Chicago gun-battle amounted to
seven shots fired by sixteen-year-old Christopher Craig from a
First World War revolver. The police had not fired back and
there were no automatic weapons. Al Capone or Machine-
Gun Kelly might have thought it rather tame.

None of this was much comfort to an unarmed police force and a civilian population that increasingly saw themselves at the mercy of the hardened young thug with an itchy trigger finger. Apart from a particular fear of the gunman, the public recognized a new type of lawlessness, increasingly violent and cocksure. Once again, the new breed of criminal had been trained in war or profited by its example. Such men were young, tough and resourceful. The burglar of the 1930s still had an air of Bill Sikes. A decade later, the hero of the young and violent criminal was more likely to have been a commando fighter in the raids on St Nazaire or Dieppe.

If any particular area of the capital was regarded as a breeding ground for violent crime, it was the terrain south of the river, beyond the wharves and warehouses from London Bridge down to Greenwich. Among their honest citizens, the bomb-scarred streets and temporary 'prefabs' of working-class housing in Bermondsey and Deptford, Lewisham and New Cross, harboured more criminals to the square mile than any other area. So it was said.

There was little reassurance from the news as the bitter winter of 1947 was followed by one of the finest and hottest summers for many years. With a gun in his hand, the young robber had no need for subtlety. On 25 April 1947, three men with scarves over the lower part of their faces burst into a jeweller's shop in the busy Bayswater street of Queensway. They held up the staff, looted the premises and got clean away in a stolen car that had been parked outside. Such a car was generally stolen just before the robbery so that its owner would have had no chance to alert the police to its loss. If there was an answer to crime that happened so randomly and unpredictably, it had yet to be found. Sir Harold Scott later wrote that he feared such criminals would, at will, 'shoot their way in and out after the manner of a gangster film'.

Public anxiety and outrage over such incidents grew. Combined with the philosophy of 'All pull together and we'll pull the country through', it inspired a mood of defiance or desperation in which the individual citizen might take the law into his own hands. Horace Walpole's account of the Piccadilly hold-up two centuries earlier would have suggested to his readers that such reckless courage was likely to have fatal consequences. The truth of this was all too soon apparent.

2

By 29 April 1947, the last of winter had given way to warm spring. At midday, the little cafés of the central London thoroughfare of Charlotte Street were busy with shop and office workers in their Tuesday lunch-hour. There was also heavy traffic on this route between Oxford Street and Euston Road. Charlotte Street runs parallel to Tottenham Court Road and just to its west. Tottenham Street, with its plain-faced façades of London brick with greengrocers or newsagents at street level, ran from Tottenham Court Road, crossing Charlotte Street and continuing west towards Upper Regent Street.

During the blitz, a bomb had demolished the premises on the northwest corner of the Charlotte Street and Tottenham Street crossing. Next to this empty site was a one-storey survival of the original buildings with a distinctly temporary look to it. Above the blackened brick of the front was a signboard: 'Jays the Jewellers'. The little shop looked more like a pawnbroker's premises, which it also was, than the conventional Bond Street image of a West End jewellers. A plain wooden sign hanging over a shabby door discreetly announced 'Pledge Entrance'.

By about 2.30 p.m., when the crowds had gone back to work, the sixty-year-old managing director of Jays, Alfred Stock, had returned from lunch. He unlocked the door of the large safe to put away some items. Behind him, as he did so, there were rings to the value of £2000 in the showcases – about eight years' income for the average worker. Also in the shop was the manager, Bert Keates, who was ten years older than Mr Stock. Neither man had any reason to notice the rather square and black pre-war Vauxhall 14 saloon car crossing Charlotte Street and pulling up outside the shop. Nor had they noticed the passer-by just before, as he peered through the window and saw the display of rings with only two old men serving in the shop.

A moment later the shop door burst open and a scene of gangster-movie unreality began. Three young men entered with scarves over the lower part of their faces and revolvers in their hands. One of the young men shouted, 'This is a stick-up! Get 'em up and keep quiet!' Another of the raiders leapt the counter, making for the safe. As he did so, Mr Stock slammed the safe door shut, so that it automatically locked. The young man who had leapt the counter shouted at Mr Stock for the keys. Mr Stock made no movement. The young man grappled with him, knocked him to the ground and began to club the old man's head with his revolver.

In the shop itself, Bert Keates picked up a stool and threw it at one of the other masked raiders. It missed, but the man fired back. In turn, he missed Mr Keates and the bullet embedded itself in the woodwork of the shop.

The explosion of the gun now brought assistants from the rear of the premises. There were six of them in all, including a woman. Someone set off the burglar alarm. Mr Stock and his assailant were still struggling on the floor by the safe. One of the other masked men shouted, 'It's too hot! I'm scramming!'

The third gunman threw his revolver at the assistants who had appeared behind the counter. At this point, pushing Mr Keates aside as he tried to grapple with one of them, the three raiders fled through the door into the street and jumped into the Vauxhall car. A customer who entered witnessed the confusion in the shop and ran out after them, shouting, 'Police! Police! Stop them!'

The scene outside was no less confused than it had been in the shop. The engine of the Vauxhall car started but, before it could move, a passing lorry driver saw the commotion. He drove his lorry across the path of the car, blocking it in. At this point, the car driver evidently tried to reverse down Tottenham Street. But the car merely jumped backwards and the gears jammed. The three men scrambled out, still wearing scarves across their faces and two of them still waving guns. They began to run down Tottenham Street in single file, back in the direction of Tottenham Court Road. As they reached the Charlotte Street crossing, a motor-cyclist was coming towards them, down Charlotte Street from the north. At the sight of the three men waving guns at the crowd as they ran and, hearing the alarm bell, he swerved towards the pavement, turned his bike across it and switched off the engine, one foot on the ground.

Events were now measured in split seconds. The three men who had been about to turn into Charlotte Street, saw their path blocked by the motor-cyclist. Their leader, without hesitation or warning, raised his revolver and shot the motor-cyclist in the head at point-blank range. As the wounded man fell, the raiders turned back along Tottenham Street, running for the Tottenham Court Road. Among the bystanders was Charles Grimshaw, an accountant. As the three men passed him, he managed to trip the second one, who fell to the pavement, his gun clattering clear. Mr Grimshaw leapt on him and they began to struggle. At this point, one of the other raiders turned back and kicked Charles Grimshaw in the head. His assailant broke away, scrambled up, snatched up the gun and pointed it at Mr Grimshaw, shouting, 'Keep away!'

The men ran on, turning into Charlotte Mews. Finding this was a cul-de-sac, they ran back, disappearing down Tottenham Street into Tottenham Court Road.

The motor-cyclist, Alec d'Antiquis, lay in Charlotte Street, his body in the roadway, his head pillowed on the edge of the pavement, his lips covered by blood that had dried black. The bullet had entered his head between the left temple and the eyebrow. To those who comforted him, the dying man said, 'I'm all right. Stop them. I did my best.' Then he lost consciousness. He was thirty-four years old, married with six children. With his war-service gratuity, he had started a motorcycle repair business in Colliers Wood, in southwest London. No one could question his public spirit. He had recently run into the roadway to stop a bolting horse and had once rescued a child from a burning house.

The first policeman to reach the scene took off his jacket and covered the fallen man with it for warmth. There seemed little more that could be done for him. An ambulance arrived and Antiquis was lifted into it. He died about ten minutes after reaching the nearby Middlesex Hospital. Divisional Inspector Bob Higgins took immediate charge of the investigation and alerted Scotland Yard.

3

Chief Inspector Robert Fabian, 'Fabian of the Yard', returned to his Whitehall office from lunch at the Colonial Club. Forty-five years old, a veteran of murder investigations and the Flying Squad, he had a formidable reputation and a gentle manner. The gentleness went with courage and resolve. Among other forms of recognition, he had been awarded the King's Police Medal for defusing an IRA bomb in Piccadilly. In April 1947, he was deputizing for his superior, Superintendent Tom Barratt of the Neville Heath case, who was then on holiday. Fabian returned from lunch just in time to be told by Inspector Bob Higgins that there had been 'a nasty job in Charlotte Street'. Antiquis was in hospital and 'going to die'.

Fabian ordered the Yard's photographic department to Charlotte Street, as well as the divisional surgeon and Superintendent Fred Cherrill, the foremost fingerprint expert.

Within hours the extent of Fabian's difficulties was plain. There were no fingerprints on the Vauxhall 14 saloon, which had been stolen from Charlotte Street itself immediately before the attempted robbery. There were no fingerprints in the shop. There were prints on the gun that one of the raiders had thrown at the assistants, but they matched none the Yard had on file. The Forensic Science Laboratory at Hendon used a micro-camera on the car's upholstery and reported, 'There isn't a shred of a clue.'

On the evening of the murder, Fabian attended Sir Bernard Spilsbury's post-mortem on the body of the murder victim. The bullet that killed Antiquis was retrieved and later identified as having been fired by a .320 calibre centre-fire revolver. The bullet in the woodwork of the shop had been fired by a revolver of .455 calibre. As for the revolver which one of the raiders had thrown at the assistants, this was already available. The gunsmith Robert Churchill reported that it was loaded with such a variety of ammunition that it was impossible to fire it at all.

The raid was hardly the most professional operation. It had the stamp of amateurism everywhere, which infinitely multiplied the number of possible suspects. Fabian was inclined to think it might have been the work of deserters on the run from the Military Police.

If modern science was of little use, old-fashioned evidence seemed worse. There had been twenty-three witnesses to the crime, all of whom gave statements to Bob Higgins. Fabian read them with dismay. 'Three enormous men ... Three dodgy little fellows ... I think one was lame ... They all ran like blazes ... All wearing raincoats ... They wore battledress jackets ... Definitely foreigners, swarthy ... They were blond and wore no hats ... Caps pulled down over their eyes ...'

It seemed hopeless. A good deal had happened in Charlotte Street that afternoon but the time had been measured in seconds rather than minutes. There was at least a chance that the killer – or killers – of Alec d'Antiquis would never be caught.

Fabian set up the headquarters of the murder investigation at Tottenham Court Road police station. Three days later, without sleep, he had got no further with it when a young man in a black leather jacket walked in, came up to the desk and asked, 'Do you want to know anything about two young fellows I saw disappear into a building off the Tottenham Court Road – just after the murder? They had handkerchiefs knotted round their chins.' Handkerchiefs or scarves, there seemed no doubt who the men must be.

The young man in the black leather jacket was Albert Grubb, a taxi-driver. He had been driving a fare along Tottenham Court Road just after 2.30 p.m. on 29 April. Though his flag was down, a man with what he first thought was a bandage round his chin jumped on the running-board as the traffic came to a halt. Then Mr Grubb thought it was not a bandage but a handkerchief. Albert Grubb shouted at him that he was booked and pointed at the flag. The man muttered something and jumped off.

The taxi-driver saw the man and a companion go into a block of offices, Brook House, 191 Tottenham Court Road. He also saw them come out again soon afterwards. One of the men had a raincoat when he entered the building but did not have it when he came out again. It was late in the day when Fabian heard this story and by then Brook House was locked up for the night. Next morning he and Bob Higgins were in a Flying Squad car, parked outside as dawn broke, 'snoozing with coat collars turned up'.

The first arrival was a porter, Leonard Joel. He knew nothing about the two men in the building on Tuesday afternoon but recalled a little key he had found while sweeping up on Thursday. When it was produced, Fabian ordered one of his men to try it in the ignition of the stolen Vauxhall. It fitted.

The next arrival at Brook House was an office boy, Brian Cox. The lad knew nothing about the key but he remembered that he had been standing in the doorway of the building on the afternoon of the previous Tuesday, 29 April. He thought it was shortly before 3 p.m. Two men had brushed past him as they came in. The taller was wearing a raincoat. They went up the stairs and he saw them looking out of the windows from time to time. They were on a stairway as he went up soon afterwards, one of them sitting on a window ledge and the other leaning against the wall. One of them asked him if 'a Mr Williams was in'. The boy said that he did not know any Mr Williams. He remembered that the taller of the two men was no longer wearing a raincoat.

As a bonus, there had been a delivery driver, Percy Skinner, at the door of Brook House when the boy saw the two men go in. Traced by the police, Mr Skinner also remembered seeing one of the men in a raincoat and later seeing him without it.

There were now at least four witnesses, the office boy, the taxi-driver and passenger, and the delivery driver, who had seen the two suspects without scarves across their faces. For the first time, there was a thread which might connect the hunters with their prey. In the next few hours, Scotland Yard officers searched Brook House with meticulous care. At last, having worked their way up without success, they reached the top floor. There was a painter's lumber-room among its offices. Behind a dusty counter, someone had stuffed a bundle of clothing. There was a raincoat, a cap and a scarf folded into a triangle with its ends knotted together.

This was not so much the best evidence as the only evidence of importance in four days of the murder hunt. It was something of an anti-climax when Fabian examined the lining of the coat and cap. In both cases the maker's name had been cut out. But while this might make identification difficult, it confirmed again that these clothes had been used in the course of the crime.

The day after the murder, Sir Harold Scott had called a conference of senior officers at Scotland Yard. He warned them that it was now or never that armed crime of the sort that had killed Antiquis must be stamped out, whatever the price. His reputation, as well as that of the entire Metropolitan Police, was at stake in the case. On his orders, every CID officer in the capital who was not engaged on urgent duties was to be assigned to the investigation. The

Commissioner then issued a public statement that anyone prepared to give information about the killers would receive full police protection. It was an admission of how little evidence the police had gathered. It was also an invitation to the underworld to hand over its rogue elements for justice. At one point, it was claimed that four thousand officers were involved in the investigation in one way or another. The principal way seemed to be in maintaining pressure on the routine activities of minor criminals, as well as watching their clubs and pubs. Sooner or later, the underworld would regard the killers as a greater nuisance to its own ranks than to the general public. At that point, someone might talk.

But no one talked. Fabian and his officers turned to matters of evidence.

4

The raincoat found at Brook House was of the commonest kind, a light fawn mackintosh lined inside with tartan weave. It was a type worn by millions of men in the late 1940s. The grey cap, gloves and scarf found with it offered still less hope of identification. However, the raincoat was taken to the Forensic Science Laboratory at Hendon. Surely if it had been worn by one of the killers, there would be some clue, somewhere. To Fabian's chagrin, the Tottenham Court Road teleprinter chattered out a message from the forensic scientists. 'Regret no identification in raincoat, cap, scarf or gloves.' The trail had gone cold, abruptly and perhaps finally.

Like tens of thousands of similar raincoats, this one had been made in Leeds by Montague Burton for distribution to the firm's retail stores in almost every town and city in the land. That was not much help. On a hunch, Fabian ordered the garment to be unstitched. Surely, there might be something, perhaps in the lining, which would help to identify its owner. There was nothing of that kind, but inside one of the seams was sewn a maker's cloth stock-ticket with a number on it, 7800. Fabian sent this at once to Montague Burton in Leeds by police car. The message that came back was again disappointing. The firm's records showed that the coat had gone to one of its branches in the London area. Fabian persisted. Which area? The reply to this was that it had probably gone to Montague Burton in Bermondsey or the firm's shop in Deptford High Street. The high-powered Railton squad car set off for Deptford High Street.

At last it seemed that the quarry might be in view. In 1947 it was still impossible to buy clothes legally without clothing coupons, which were issued in a ration book. In the case of clothing coupons, as with petrol coupons, there was a thriving black market trade in printing forgeries. It was less sophisticated than forging bank notes and, in its way, almost as profitable. Because of the widespread forgeries, tailors and outfitters shops were in the habit of noting down the name on the ration card from which they cut the coupons when clothes were bought. Montague Burton in Deptford High Street, like the other shops visited in the murder hunt, had a record of the names of those who had bought raincoats from them in the last year or so.

Fabian scanned the list of names from this and other Montague Burton stores in the London area. None of them matched those of known criminals. Customers were visited who all proved law-abiding and had genuine alibis for 29 April. Yet there was one name that no one seemed able to account for, though it matched no criminal record: Kemp Thomas. The raincoat had been bought at Montague Burton in Deptford High Street on 30 December 1946. Fabian had been staring at the name for some time before he realized what was wrong. He was reading names that had been copied down in the wrong order. On Robert Fabian's own clothing coupon book, his name appeared as Fabian, Robert. The shop assistant at Montague Burton in Deptford High Street had written the names exactly as they appeared on the card. Putting the two names the other way round, Fabian recognized them. Thomas Kemp was not a criminal. However, he was related by marriage to another man with an impressive criminal record, his brother-in-law. This realization was not so much a feat of memory on Fabian's part as the fruit of twenty-five years' daily experience of the London underworld.

He checked with the shop and confirmed the address, a tenement block, Park Buildings, Bermondsey. The wife of the man who had bought the raincoat was at home. Fabian showed the raincoat to her and asked if it belonged to her husband. Vera Kemp said that it looked like his but that he had lost it at a public house about five weeks earlier. Fabian appeared to be satisfied. He went back to the car and drove off. But before entering Park Buildings, he had positioned another officer to watch the woman's movements. As his car disappeared, Mrs Kemp came out and was trailed to another block of flats. She was there for some time and then went home. Fabian's man was able to see which flat she had visited. It was let to a family named Jenkins.

The name was ordinary enough, but two members of the family had a special place in the records of Scotland Yard. An elder brother, Thomas Jenkins, was serving an eight-year sentence for manslaughter. This followed a lunchtime smash-and-grab raid on a jeweller's shop in Birchin Lane, in the financial district of the City of London, in 1944. A naval officer, Captain Ralph Binney, had stepped out into the middle of the road to block the path of the getaway car. The car drove straight at him, knocking him over and trapping him underneath, dragging him under the car down Lombard Street to the river, over London Bridge, and down Tooley Street where he was thrown clear. He died three hours later from his injuries and the Binney Medal for civilian bravery in assisting the police was instituted in memory of his courage. One of those in the car was Thomas Jenkins.

Thomas Jenkins was still serving his prison sentence and could not have been involved in the murder of Alec d'Antiquis. His younger brother, twenty-three-year-old Charles Henry Jenkins, had a criminal record of his own and was a member of the same gang, which called itself 'The Elephant Boys'. This derived from a racecourse and protection racket of the 1920s and 1930s, the self-styled Elephant Gang of Monkey Benneyworth, 'The Trimmer', and Georgie Sewell. The Elephant and Castle thugs had fought a long war with fist and razor against Darby Sabini's gang from Clerkenwell's 'Little Italy'. But that was over. The Elephant Boys now drank in pubs that were once forbidden territory, the Three Tuns or the Griffin on the south side of Clerkenwell Road.

Henry Jenkins had been known to the police since childhood. Apart from anything else, he had two convictions for assaulting the police and had broken one policeman's jaw. He was known as 'The King of Borstal' and had only been released from his last sentence on 23 April 1947, six days before the killing of Alec d'Antiquis. He had held a coming-out party at the Griffin.

It was now 11 May, twelve days after the murder. The evidence began to take shape. It did so with a neatness that seemed almost too good to be true.

Thomas Kemp was picked up before he reached home that night, driven to Tottenham Court Road police station and questioned by Fabian. He said that he had been unable to find his raincoat the previous week. He thought he had left it at the cinema. 'Your wife said you lost it in a public house,' Fabian said. 'Who's making the mistake?' 'We both are,' Kemp conceded. 'She lent it to her brother, Henry Jenkins.'

Fabian decided that this was sufficient evidence to arrest Henry Jenkins. He and his men drove to Bermondsey next day, on Sunday morning 12 May, sealed off the flat and rang the bell. When Jenkins came to the door, Fabian said simply, 'Come on. We want you inside.' Jenkins came quietly. With the church bells ringing he was driven to Tottenham Court Road and shown the raincoat. 'It looks like Tom's coat,' he said, 'but I'm not saying any more now as it all looks serious to me.' That was that. Henry Jenkins would say no more.

The suspect was put in a cell while his known associates were checked and some of them brought in for questioning. A boy of seventeen, Terence Rolt, said that he had been ill on 29 April and had spent the day in bed. Twenty-year-old Christopher Geraghty came to the police station of his own accord, when Fabian had failed to find him, and volunteered the information that he had been suffering from boils and was housebound on 29 April. Like the others, these two interviewees were released.

Henry Jenkins remained crucial to Fabian's case. Despite his ugly reputation, he was a young man of striking appearance with fair curly hair and what was then called 'dashing' good looks. A 'young corsair', was Fabian's description. But Jenkins refused to talk and the evidence against him was slight. Contrary to the hackneyed image of solidarity among a close-knit criminal fraternity, there were a good many grudges being paid off among members of the so-called 'Elephant Boys'. Trust among members of the neighbourhood gang had gone the way of all good things. Was it impossible that, even if Jenkins ever had the raincoat, someone had purloined it for the raid and discarded it when the plan went wrong? There was one answer to this and to all other doubts in the case. The one decisive piece of evidence against Jenkins or an accomplice would be identification. Having discarded the doubtful ones, Fabian had twenty-seven witnesses who had seen the gunmen, four of them having seen the men without masks. Fabian called in all the men and women who swore, as he put it, that 'they could identify any of the three gunmen they had glimpsed on Charlotte Street.' Indeed, those who had seen two of the suspects at Brook House had had more than a glimpse. The office boy and the delivery driver had seen those two men more than once over a period of time.

At 11 a.m. on Monday 12 May, Fabian arranged an identification parade at Tottenham Court Road police station. Jenkins consented to it. For a guilty man, the ordeal and the risk of being viewed by twenty-seven witnesses – not just one or two – was considerable. By the law of averages someone might pick him out. Fabian noticed that Jenkins had asked for a lunch-edition of a London evening paper, which came on the streets at mid-morning. The significance of this, he suggested, was that it was an old trick of the professional criminal. Jenkins had the paper folded in his jacket pocket. A witness noticing it as he or she came along the line of men would think, 'It couldn't be this man – obviously he was out on the street a few minutes ago.' But a positive witness, of whom there were twenty-seven, would surely judge by the face rather than by the pocket.

Henry Jenkins stood in a line of fair-haired men for an hour and ten minutes. He appeared relaxed and confident, like a man who has nothing to worry about. The twenty-seven witnesses went past in turn, scrutinizing each face. At the end of the line each witness was asked whether any suspect seen in the Charlotte Street shooting was standing in that line of men. Every one of the twenty-seven witnesses said he was not.

It seemed as if Fabian's investigation had been blown apart.

5

Henry Jenkins was released from custody, though Fabian had him tailed day and night. The suspect was followed to a familiar rendezvous, the Griffin in Clerkenwell Road, where he met Geraghty and Rolt. He had had no time to arrange such a meeting and there was nothing remarkable in the three young men making for their usual pub. It was reported that they talked quietly and looked worried. Since they had just been held and interrogated over a hanging matter, this was not surprising. On the following day, Fabian asked Jenkins and his sister to come to Tottenham Court Road police station and make statements about the raincoat. That afternoon, in the interview room, Fabian sat on one side of the table and the two interviewees on the other. Jenkins said to his sister, as though giving in reluctantly, 'Let's tell Mr Fabian who I lent the coat to.' He paused and lit a cigarette. Fabian noticed that the young man's fingers were steady and the flame of the match did not flicker. Then came the name. Bill Walsh.

William Henry Walsh was well-known. He had a long criminal record and had only recently been released from prison. 'We saw him about a week ago in Southend,' Vera Kemp said. 'He's knocking about with a blonde girl who works in a café on the front. If you go to Southend, it would interest you to go to number thirty-two. I don't know the name of the road.' Fabian was taken aback by this betrayal, which seemed quite out of keeping with the Jenkins's code of loyalty. Yet it rather neatly matched another piece of information.

While following the line of inquiry from Brook House to Bermondsey, Fabian had remained alert to possible links between the robbery at the shop in Queensway on 15 April, which had netted £4517 in plate and jewellery, and the fracas in Charlotte Street four days later. What was the story in the underworld about the Queensway robbery? If anyone knew the answer, it was likely to be the Divisional Detective Inspector at Tottenham Court Road, Fred Hodge. Hodge replied that he had an informant who was 'singing his head off' about William Walsh as one of the men in the Queensway raid. It was said that he had gone to Southend to fence the proceeds of the robbery. There was no proof of this, but the story now acquired fresh interest.

Duncan Webb, veteran crime-reporter and deputy-editor of the Sunday *People,* was now briefed by the police that they were looking for Walsh as the leader of the gang that had attempted to rob Jays and had shot Alec d'Antiquis. Henry Jenkins, for the moment, was off the menu. Walsh was described as thirty-seven years old, looking not unlike Humphrey Bogart, usually dressed in a pin-stripe grey suit with obviously padded shoulders.

The focus of the investigation shifted abruptly to Southend and the search for the Queensway robber. The murder squad cars with armed officers set off down Eastern Avenue for the seaside resort as the May temperature climbed into the upper eighties. They reached Southend with its straggling pier and holiday crowds, its glittering quicksilver estuary of the Thames and the steamers plying across to the Medway or up to Tower Pier. Fabian headed for the police station and the Occurrences Book. In this book each officer noted occurrences while he was on the beat or on duty. They need not be crimes, just anything worthy of note. On the evening of 25 April, at 9.40, PC Frederick Jauncey reported the suspicious behaviour of two young men in a telephone kiosk. He took particulars from the wartime identity cards they were still carrying. Their names were Christopher James Geraghty and Michael Joseph Gillam. Next morning, at 7.15, PC James Gunn found a loaded .455 revolver in a shrubbery close to the pier. Southend began to seem more important than London.

Fabian and Fred Hodge searched the seafront cafés for the blonde waitress. They discovered where she lived and talked to her parents. Her father announced that Walsh had been in Southend on 25 April, the day of the Queensway robbery, with Harry Jenkins. 'Suddenly Bill Walsh seemed to disappear. Nobody knew where he'd gone. Then Jenkins said Walsh had double-crossed him, and something about getting his revenge.'

From this tangle, Fabian and Hodge guessed that Walsh and Jenkins had been two of the masked men in the Queensway robbery. Walsh had presumably double-crossed his partner by vanishing with the loot. The murder squad then had a very busy day, raiding houses in Southend, taking up floorboards, dismantling cupboards and cutting open mattresses. They visited the fence to whom Walsh was said to have sold jewellery and found two rings that had been stolen in the Queensway robbery. Six cars carrying armed police then converged on a house in South Church Avenue, where the fence thought Walsh was living with a woman named Doris Hart. The house was surrounded and armed officers burst in. Again the house was searched. There was no sign of the fugitives.

Photographs of William Henry Walsh and Doris Hart appeared in the *Police Gazette* and the national press, identified as a couple who were wanted to assist the police with their inquiries. The search was nationwide, though it concentrated on Soho, Bermondsey, Elephant and Castle, Brighton, and Southend. The Special Branch was instructed to watch all ports and airports.

Embarrassingly for the murder squad, Bill Walsh was all this time living at home with his wife in Plumstead in a post-war prefab. When told this in a phone call by the journalist Duncan Webb, Fabian's men found it laughably improbable and did nothing. On 16 May, after so much talk of armed police and shoot-outs, Walsh was arrested by a retired policeman and a bicycling constable, while sheltering from the rain under a tree on Plumstead Common. Instead of drawing a gun, he just said plaintively, 'What's all this about?' as they grabbed him.

However it happened, Fabian now had his man. But as Walsh was arrested, there were further discoveries on the muddy foreshore of the Thames at Wapping. An eight-year-old boy and his friends had been playing near the low-water mark when they found a gun. Indeed, they were playing with the gun itself when someone noticed them. It was a .320 revolver loaded with five live cartridges and one case. Three of the cartridges had misfired. Shortly afterwards a .455 Bulldog Special was found nearby, loaded with .450 ammunition which was too small to work. It contained bullets which were more than fifty years old. Robert Churchill, having test-fired the guns and compared the bullets with those found at the scene of the Charlotte Street crime, identified the .320 revolver as the murder weapon and the .455 as the gun that had fired a shot into the woodwork of the jeweller's shop.

6

Under such circumstances, Fabian began his interrogation of William Henry Walsh at Woolwich police station where the wanted man was held. Walsh began with 'a wry twisted smile' and the demand, 'What do you want me for?' Fabian's reply dented the Bogart image. 'It could be for armed robbery, Walsh – else it could be for murder. It depends on you and what you know.' For a while Walsh paced up and down, smoking. He asked for a glass of water. After it had been brought, he said, 'I can see it's serious. I'll tell you about my part in the Queensway job, but I've nothing to do with the Charlotte Street business.'

William Walsh then described the Queensway robbery, which he claimed had been carried out with Henry Jenkins, Christopher Geraghty and another man he would only call 'Joe'. Fabian guessed correctly that 'Joe' was Michael Joseph Gillam, the ex-Borstal Boy who had been seen behaving suspiciously with Geraghty in a Southend phone kiosk. Walsh admitted the Queensway robbery, the visit to Southend, and double-crossing Jenkins over the proceeds. He admitted reconnoitring Jays for Geraghty, Rolt and Jenkins, but he took no part in the raid. Indeed, he had an alibi for the time.

Walsh's statement was valuable but highly suspect as evidence in court. In itself, it was not evidence against any of those he named, since a statement made about a man in his absence is, strictly speaking, only evidence against the person making it. However, in the small hours of the following morning, 17 May, the arrests began. Christopher Geraghty was first. When told that he was to be interviewed again by Fabian, he said, 'I hope he doesn't think I'm going to open up and get a revolver in my back.'

At 2.30 a.m. it was the turn of the seventeen-year-old, Terence Rolt. He was badly shaken by the experience of being dragged from sleep by armed officers. At the police station desk, he saw Geraghty in custody and blurted out, 'I bungled it. I'll tell you what happened. Chris never meant to kill that man.' Jenkins, bundled from sleep into a Black Maria with six armed policemen, seemed unconcerned. 'Don't you guys ever sleep? Do you work night and day?' he asked wearily. Then, as the van drove through the streets, he burst into song, 'Night and day, you are the one ... You, only you, under the sun ...' He did not behave like a man who expected to be charged with murder or hanged.

Christopher Geraghty made a confession implicating himself, Rolt and another man whom he would not name. Rolt had driven, or attempted to drive, the getaway car. Geraghty himself had fired the shot in the jeweller's and also the shot that killed Antiquis. He swore that he had shot in the direction of Antiquis to frighten him off but had not intended to kill him. This was probably true since, in such circumstances, there was no advantage in killing a man if it was possible to scare him off. Legally, however, it was still murder unless grounds were found for reducing the charge to manslaughter.

Christopher Geraghty's story was of himself, Rolt, and 'that other fellow' who was not Jenkins. On the night of Saturday 26 April, they had broken into a gunsmith's in Union Street, near Borough Tube Station. They spent the night there, surveying the guns and ammunition. At noon on Sunday, they sauntered out with their haul. On Tuesday 29 April, they met outside Whitechapel Tube Station at 11 a.m. and took the underground to Goodge Street. They had decided to 'take sight' of jewellers' shops in the area of Tottenham Court Road. Rolt went to look at Jays but came back saying that he thought there was only jewellery to the value of £2000 in the shop. Geraghty went to look. He came back and suggested it was more like £5000 and worth doing. But he found too many people around in the lunch-hour crowds and suggested they should wait a little. They went to have a meal in a café.

Afterwards, Rolt and 'that other fellow' went to steal a car in Charlotte Street. With Geraghty, they drove into Tottenham Street and parked outside Jays. It seemed that Rolt misunderstood his companions and thought the raid was to begin immediately. Being next to the pavement, he got out of the car and dashed into the shop waving his gun. The others had no choice but to follow. From that moment, everything had gone wrong.

Rolt was told that Geraghty had made this statement implicating him in the murder. Rolt then made a similar statement of his own, admitting that he and Geraghty had been present at the crime. What followed next was described by Fabian in rather curious terms. 'And since Jenkins was not his heart-sworn comrade he implicated Jenkins.' There was almost a suggestion that Jenkins might not have been there. This was of crucial importance because Rolt was the only person, among witnesses or accused, who placed Jenkins in Charlotte Street. Seven other witnesses, apart from Jenkins himself, placed him in Bermondsey at the time of the murder.

It was on the evening of Monday 19 May, almost three weeks after the death of Alec d'Antiquis, that Geraghty, Jenkins and Rolt were charged with his murder. Geraghty and Jenkins, as well as Walsh and Gillam, were then charged with the robbery of the Bayswater jeweller's in Queensway.

The murder trial opened at the Old Bailey on 21 July. Russell Vick KC, for Jenkins, submitted that his client should be tried separately, since he alone denied being present at the murder, but Mr Justice Hallett refused this. Anthony Hawke KC, who had prosecuted Neville Heath the previous autumn, presented the case for the Crown. None of it was new. The witnesses told their stories. Forensic evidence was given by Sir Bernard Spilsbury and Robert Churchill, police evidence by Bob Higgins, Fred Hodge and Robert Fabian. The case for Geraghty was that he had not intended to harm Alec d'Antiquis and that he was guilty only of manslaughter. Rolt, at seventeen, was too young to face the death penalty.

Only Russell Vick for Henry Jenkins had a defence that might succeed and he put his client into the witness box. It was all or nothing. If Jenkins was present at the murder, then it was the prosecution argument that he and Rolt were the two men who had hidden in Brook House. The office boy had talked to him, face to face. It was now said that the gunmen's scarves had begun to slip down their faces as they ran. In that case, many more of the witnesses would have had a good look at them. Not one of the twenty-seven witnesses identified Jenkins as having been present at the scene of the murder. Whatever the truth of the borrowed raincoat, if he was not one of the three men in Charlotte Street, he did not take part in the crime.

Against this was the story told by William Walsh, who had already double-crossed Jenkins in any case. But it was not evidence. Walsh was not there and could only report what he knew by hearsay. There was also the statement by Rolt, who named Jenkins as one of the robbers. But the uncorroborated word of a self-confessed participant in the crime seemed scarcely enough to hang a man. What inducements might have been offered or what persuasion employed during questioning?

The prosecution case against Henry Jenkins was not weak, nor was it conclusive. Unlike his co-defendants, much depended on his own testimony. In the witness box, he described how he had been with his sister at work on 29 April from 10 a.m. to 4 p.m. This was not Vera Kemp, the sister whose husband had lent the raincoat, but another sister, Mrs Burns. Six other people had seen him there during the day. These six witnesses duly gave their evidence. Henry Jenkins's alibi was not shaken, let alone broken. It was complete.

He withstood cross-examination and scored at least one important point off Anthony Hawke. He was asked how he knew, when Fabian showed him the raincoat, that it had anything to do with the murder. Jenkins said that Fabian had told him so. This was challenged and Jenkins was accused of lying. But then the record was checked. Fabian had indeed said in evidence to the court that he told Jenkins the raincoat was found where two men ran off after a shooting in Charlotte Street.

The judge reminded the jury that where three men committed a crime in the course of which a man was killed, as Antiquis had been, it mattered not whose finger pulled the trigger. All were equally guilty. As for the plea of manslaughter, where an escaping felon prevents a private person from stopping him, 'the felon does so at his own risk and is guilty of murder if that violent measure results even unintentionally in the death of the victim.'

The jury were out for less than an hour. They returned verdicts of guilty against all three defendants. Jenkins and Geraghty were sentenced to death. Rolt, because of his youth, was sentenced to be detained during His Majesty's pleasure. He was released from prison in 1955. At a trial in October, William Walsh and Michael Gillam were to be sent to prison for the Queensway robbery, which they had carried out with Jenkins and Geraghty. After their appeals in the murder case had been dismissed, Henry Jenkins and

Christopher Geraghty were hanged at Pentonville prison on 19 September 1947.

The verdicts and death sentences drew mingled relief and misgiving. Robert Fabian and others saw them as a check to the spread and use of guns by the young post-war thug. For several weeks after it was announced that Jenkins and Geraghty had been hanged, discarded guns were to be found, 'abandoned in parks under bushes, in dustbins, dropped through the floors of bombed houses, fished up by Thames River patrolmen in nets from the low-tide mud. The men of the underworld had decided to think twice about using guns in London.'

It was a famous victory – or was it? In some quarters there were protests at the sentences because of the youth of the two men, Jenkins twenty-three and Geraghty twenty. Capital punishment was temporarily abandoned the following year between a vote of the House of Commons to abolish it and a vote of the House of Lords upholding it. In the case of Jenkins, there were other misgivings. Of all the independent witnesses to the crime, not one identified him as a participant. Jenkins was a striking-looking young man, if not a handsome one. The other men in the line-up were fair-haired but not look-alikes. His alibi was also well supported. Against it was the evidence of one co-accused and a story at second-hand from a self-confessed robber of the Queensway jeweller's.

Was it his reputation that hanged him? He was a Borstal Boy and a thug, though not an armed robber. He was a very likely suspect. There was a story in the underworld that he had been in Charlotte Street, following an agreement at his coming-out party from Borstal on 23 June. He, Geraghty and Rolt were hard up. It would be simple to rob a jeweller's by walking in, brandishing a gun, and snatching the goods on display. Such was the rumour in the underworld and, of course, Fabian set great store by what the underworld was saying. But there was not a shred of proof to support this story which had, in any case, been planted by Walsh, Jenkins's arch-enemy after 24 April.

The possibilities were 1) that Jenkins could show himself innocent; 2) that neither his innocence nor his guilt could be established beyond doubt; 3) that his guilt could be conclusively shown. There were many people who believed that neither the first nor the third of these propositions had been demonstrated. The second had an attraction, both for the soft-hearted and some unlikely members of the hard-boiled. Duncan Webb of the *People* reviewed the case. His sources extended to murder squad officers and to areas of the underworld that would talk in confidence to Webb but never to the police. He concluded cryptically of Henry Jenkins, 'Even after his trial, he still pleaded that he was not present when Antiquis was murdered.... It would never surprise me if Jenkins was telling the truth when he said that.'

Duncan Webb had seen the trial and the evidence for himself. Against one witness and one hearsay statement, there were twenty-seven independent witnesses and seven alibi witnesses. That Jenkins was hanged in error might be a question rather than an assertion but, to Webb, it was a question never answered by those who might have done so.

6 'I Wouldn't Do a Thing Like That.' (1961)

1

The A6 murder case of 1961 offered two incompatible accounts of the crime. That was not unusual. In this case, however, each account was well-supported on evidence and yet each was flawed. If one version of events prevailed, the door to freedom was open for the young man in the dock. If the other was accepted, the only path from the dock led to the execution chamber. Perhaps it was unfortunate for James Hanratty that English law had never adopted the Scottish verdict of 'not proven'.

Most murders are quickly solved and are characteristically the work of those with no criminal record, driven to kill by domestic circumstances or by personal greed, envy, rage, sexual passion or obsession. Almost anyone might be a murderer in those terms. Murders are also committed, or sometimes alleged to be committed, by those whose trade is crime. Dishonesty, prevarication and falsehood are tools of that trade. Not surprisingly, these are the judicial decisions most likely to be questioned. Does a jury more readily convict a man because it knows he has a record of theft or deceit?

Men like John Williams, Neville Heath, Walter Rowland, Henry Jenkins and James Hanratty had criminal records, not always for crimes of violence. They were, of course, innocent of murder until proved guilty. But was it right to think privately that such men were more likely to be guilty of a great crime because they had shown few scruples about committing lesser ones? Or was it more sensible to allow for the fact that when cornered they were likely to lie and shift and prevaricate, as naturally as other men might say nothing and demand to see a solicitor? Were they, even if innocent, their own worst enemies? It was a question which must surely have crossed the mind of anyone who sat through the trial of James Hanratty at Bedford Shire Hall in January and February 1962.

The A6 murder was one of the most cold-blooded and widely publicized crimes of its time. It began as an odd, almost absurd, attempt at a hold-up. It developed into a nightmare of abduction, menaces, rape, mental torment, the murder of one victim and the maiming for life of another. That it was a journey into terror might be a superfluous description, but it was none the less true.

Late in the evening of 22 August 1961, Michael John Gregsten and Valerie Storie drove in Gregsten's Morris Minor from the Old Station Inn at Taplow to the edge of a Buckinghamshire cornfield at Dorney Reach on the banks of the Thames. They had been planning a motor rally for the social club of the Road Research Laboratory at Slough, where they both worked. That Gregsten was a married man in love with Valerie Storie mattered only insofar as it was later suggested that the crime was a bungled attempt to persuade the couple to part. Yet there was no reliable evidence to support the story that an unnamed man had employed a petty criminal for this purpose.

While the couple were in the parked car, sometime between dusk and darkness, there was a tap at the driver's window. A man stood outside in a dark suit and white shirt, his head concealed. As Gregsten wound the window down, a gun was poked into the car. The stranger said, 'This is a hold-up. I am a desperate man.' He added that he was on the run and wanted food. In summary, he got into the back of the car, ordering the couple to face the front, and produced a gun which he said was a .38 and for which he had plenty of ammunition. He also said cryptically that he had never shot anyone before. Miss Storie managed to see that he was wearing black gloves, hence no fingerprints.

The man told them that he had done sentences of corrective training and preventive detention. He also said, 'Call me "Jim".' He took their wrist-watches and most of their money, though he later gave back the watches. He then handed Gregsten back the ignition keys and ordered him to drive towards Slough, having said that he wanted to get to Slough or Maidenhead. They drove past Slough towards London, stopping once for petrol. The man kept Valerie Storie hostage with the gun aimed at her while Gregsten bought the petrol. They drove on along Western Avenue towards Harrow, turning north, stopping again at Stanmore for Gregsten to get some cigarettes from a machine.

Despite the gunman's initial demand for food, he did not stop to eat. Gregsten drove on through the darkness. As he drove, he surreptitiously flashed the reversing light on and off in an attempt to attract the attention of other motorists. As one car overtook the Morris Minor, its driver made a signal to Gregsten, as if to alert him to the malfunction of the light. That was all. On the gunman's instructions they took the A5 to St Albans and then the A6 past Luton and on towards Bedford. At about 1.30 a.m. the man announced 'I want a kip,' and told Gregsten to turn off the road. They were between Luton and Bedford, at Deadman's Hill on the A6. The abductor chose a picnic site in a lay-by. Twice he ordered Gregsten to drive into it and twice Gregsten drove past and was made to return. At last he pulled in. The car was still and the lights turned off.

The couple begged the man not to shoot them. He replied that if he had wanted to shoot them, he would have done it long ago. However, since he was going to have a sleep, it would be necessary to tie them up. He used Gregsten's tie and a piece of cord to tie Valerie Storie's wrists. There was a duffle-bag in the front of the car which might contain something to tie Gregsten with. He told Gregsten to pass it to him in the back seat. As Gregsten picked up the bag and turned, the gunman seemed to sense that it was about to be thrown at him. Without warning, he fired twice, hitting Gregsten in the head with both shots and killing him instantly.

So easily did murder spring from an apparently motiveless, aimless, and half-absurd hi-jack. Valerie Storie screamed, turned to the gunman and shouted, 'You bastard! You shot him! Why did you shoot him? You promised me you would not shoot!' 'He frightened me,' the gunman said. 'He moved too quick. I got frightened.'

She pleaded with him to get a doctor, believing that

Gregsten might still be alive, though his blood was running down between the seat and the side of the car. 'Be quiet will you?' the gunman said. 'I am thinking.' Or rather, as she recalled, he said, 'I am finking.'

The nightmare of the woman alone began when he ordered her to turn in her seat and kiss him. At last she did so and saw his face properly for the first time, illuminated by the headlights of a passing car. Then he ordered her to get out of the front of the car and into the back. He made her remove her underwear and lie on the back seat of the car, where he raped her. The body of Michael Gregsten was slumped in the driving seat, not two feet away, the face thoughtfully covered with a cloth by the killer.

After this, the assailant made the young woman lift the dead body of her lover from the car, holding it under the arm-pits as she dragged it round behind the vehicle and laid it on the ground. Since it was plain that Michael Gregsten was dead, she begged the man to take the car and go. 'There is no hurry,' he said. But as the short summer night moved close to daybreak, it seems he judged it best to be on his way. He asked the young woman to start the car for him and show him where the gears were. She had to show him how the gears worked twice before he managed to get the hang of them. On the first occasion that he tried them, the engine cut out and she had to start the car for him again. He also asked where the switches for the lights were and how they worked. Since he had just watched someone else drive the Morris Minor for several hours, his present incompetence suggested that he had had little experience of cars or their use.

He was some six to eight feet from the young woman when, without warning, he raised the gun and fired several shots. Four bullets hit her and she fell over, feeling, as she later said, that she had lost the use of her legs. There was a pause as he reloaded and fired again into the darkness. This time she heard the bullets pass over her. She lay still, pretending to be dead, as he walked over and looked down at her. He pushed her with his foot and seemed satisfied that the two volleys of bullets had done their work. Presently, the car drove away. The injured woman lay there for about three hours as daylight came. Before losing consciousness, she evidently tried to arrange some small stones beside her into letters, forming the words, 'Blue eyes and brown hair.'

Valerie Storie and Michael Gregsten were found by a labourer at about 6.45 a.m. He called John Kerr, an Oxford undergraduate taking part in a road census as a temporary job during the long vacation. While waiting for the police and the ambulance, John Kerr wrote down a partial description of the gunman from Valerie Storie's words on the back of a traffic census form. 'Staring eyes, light, fairish hair.' The first police vehicle arrived in less than twenty minutes. Valerie Storie had been dreadfully injured by the bullets and, though she was to live, she was paralyzed permanently from the waist down.

2

As the investigation began, Valerie Storie was able to describe to the police the events of her nightmare car journey in considerable detail. By that evening of 23 August 1961, as the biggest murder hunt in British criminal history began, the press issued the first descriptions of the wanted man. He was about thirty years old, five feet six inches tall, medium build, wearing a dark lounge suit. He had a pale face, deep-set brown eyes, dark hair and a London East End accent. Both the colour of the eyes and that of the hair had changed since the first tentative account. His crime seemed to be a case of random theft or robbery leading to murder. He would surely repeat it, unless he was caught.

Superintendent Robert Acott of Scotland Yard led the murder inquiry. The first development came later that day when the Morris Minor was found abandoned near Redbridge tube station in east London, some twelve hours after the discovery of the crime. There were two cartridge cases in the car. On the following day, a .38 Enfield revolver with sixty rounds of ammunition was found hidden in the space under a back seat on the upper deck of a 36A London Transport bus, which ran north-to-south between Kilburn High Road and Peckham. The gun had recently been fired and was identified as the weapon which had killed Michael Gregsten and maimed Valerie Storie. There were no fingerprints on it and nothing to indicate who might have owned it.

On the same day, 24 August, three witnesses came

forward. James Trower had seen a car, which he believed to be the Morris Minor, grinding its gears as it turned a corner at about 7.15 a.m. on 23 August near the place where it was found abandoned. John Skillett and Edward Blackhall had almost been involved in a collision with a car they identified positively as Michael Gregsten's. It had swerved in and out of the lanes of a dual carriageway at traffic lights. As they drew level again, Mr Blackhall wound down the passenger window and Mr Skillett shouted at the other driver, 'Are you fucking mad or something? You ought to get off the fucking road!' The other driver turned and laughed at him before driving on.

Two identikit pictures were issued, one based on Valerie Storie's description and the second on those of other witnesses. But that was as far as the case progressed for more than another fortnight. The next development occurred at the Vienna Hotel in the long drab stretch of Sutherland Avenue, Maida Vale. The manager of the hotel was checking Room 24, a large room in the basement, not in constant use. In an upholstered chair, he discovered two cartridge cases. Instead of throwing them away, which would probably have put an end to the murder inquiry, he phoned the police. The cartridge cases belonged to the gun which had killed Michael Gregsten.

Room 24 at the Vienna Hotel had last been used on 30 August by a man who was soon proved to have nothing to do with the crime. Previously, it had been occupied on the night before the murder by James Ryan of 72 Wood Lane, Kingsbury. A curiosity of the Vienna Hotel was one of its guests on the night of the murder. He had called himself Frederick Durrant and he had occupied Room 6 while Room 24 was unused. Frederick Durrant was an alias of Peter Louis Alphon. In the days following the murder, hotels and boarding houses had been asked to report any guest who might be a suspect in the A6 murder case. Alphon had behaved so oddly at another hotel in Finsbury Park that it was thought he might be in hiding from the law. The police were called and Alphon was asked to account for his movements on the night of the killing. A second statement by William Nudds, who worked as assistant manager at the Vienna Hotel, revealed that though Alphon stayed in Room 6 on the night of the murder, he had first been given Room 24.

It might all have seemed a matter of coincidence, except that Alphon was later to confess to the A6 murder on more than one occasion.

James Ryan had occupied Room 6 at the Vienna Hotel on the night before the murder. As James Hanratty, twenty-five years old, he was well-known to the police.

3

James Hanratty was to write his own epitaph. 'Though I am a bit of a crook, I wouldn't hurt a mouse.' Whether he would have robbed a mouse was another matter. He was a self-confessed professional burglar and car-thief, his habitat the streets and suburbs of north London, though he travelled more widely to dispose of the proceeds of theft, including visits to North Wales and Liverpool. Though he regarded himself as a professional criminal, his incompetence may be judged from the fact that he had spent most of the years 1955–61 in prison. It was said that at school he could neither read nor write, but this seemed not to be the case in his twenties. He was quite sharp, if not of great formal intelligence, and showed an ability to think on his feet. His reputation was not that of a violent man and he was not yet the prime suspect in the A6 murder inquiry.

After the discovery of the cartridge cases at the Vienna Hotel, it was not Hanratty but Peter Alphon whom Superintendent Acott named as the wanted man. Alphon was also wanted for an alleged attack and attempted rape on a woman at Richmond, on 7 September, more than a fortnight after the A6 crime. She said he had attacked her shouting, 'I am the A6 killer!' Though he escaped from the scene, she subsequently attended an identification parade and picked him out.

On 22 September, Alphon was named in the press, on radio and television as the man whom police were seeking to 'assist them with their inquiries'. The implication was quite plain to the journalists covering the investigation and the phrase used was the time-honoured description of a man the police believed guilty of the crime. So far as Scotland Yard was concerned, Alphon was the A6 murderer. Superintendent Acott had already checked Alphon's alibi, that he had spent the evening of 22 August with his mother. Mrs Alphon said that her son had spent an evening with her. It might have been 22 August or the evening before, or the evening after. This was something less than a watertight alibi.

Shortly before midnight on 22 September, a month after the murder, Alphon phoned two national newspapers. He told them that he was in a phone box outside Cannon Row police station and was about to confront Scotland Yard. For the rest of that night he was interrogated. Finally, he was put on an identification parade before Valerie Storie in her hospital bed. She picked out another man. Her distress, when she discovered this, was evident. Later, she said that there was 'a fair resemblance' between Alphon and the A6 murderer but that was not good enough. The fact that she picked out another man, rather than saying that no one on the parade looked like the killer, was perhaps the result of time having elapsed. It was now a month since she had seen her assailant by the headlights of other cars. The only change in her own description of him was when she altered the colour of his eyes from brown to blue on 31 August.

With the elimination of Alphon at the identification parade, suspicion turned to James Hanratty, who was nowhere to be found. William Nudds, assistant manager of the Vienna Hotel and by this time a self-confessed liar, made a third statement, in which he exonerated Alphon and implicated Hanratty. While the hunt was going on, however, Hanratty had been to Ireland for a week and was now back in London, lying low. On 5 October at the Rehearsal Club in Soho, he learned that he was now the chief suspect for the A6 murder. With the change of description to 'blue staring eyes', that certainly matched Hanratty rather than Alphon. To make matters worse, his friend Charles 'Dixie' France, a former doorman at the club, had told the police that Hanratty once said the back seat on the top deck of a bus was a good place to hide things. But Hanratty had been talking about worthless items from a robbery, not about guns and ammunition. He insisted that he had never owned nor used a gun.

On 6 October, Hanratty made his first untraced phone call to Scotland Yard and the *Daily Mirror*, protesting his innocence. He told Superintendent Acott where his clothes could be found and taken for forensic examination. He had been in Liverpool at the time of the murder. He had gone there to dispose of stolen goods. Unfortunately, his alibi witnesses were petty criminals like himself and they refused to incriminate themselves by coming forward.

On the evening of 6 October, Hanratty was still on the run. He went to *South Pacific* at the Dominion Theatre, Tottenham Court Road. Afterwards, he found a parked Jaguar Mark 7 in Portland Place, took its dashboard number and had an ignition key cut immediately in Soho. He came back and drove the Mark 7 from London to Manchester. There he abandoned the car and caught a train to Liverpool. He phoned Acott again from Liverpool, saying that he was trying to find witnesses and to establish his alibi for 22 August.

Every policeman in the northwest of England was looking for James Hanratty by 7 October. At 11 p.m. on 11 October, he was arrested as he came out of the Stevonia Café, Blackpool.

Carol France, Charles France's eldest daughter, had dyed Hanratty's hair dark at the beginning of August. By the time of his arrest he looked, so far as his hair might be described, like something out of a circus. His hair was naturally fair and had been dyed dark brown two months before. Now it had been dyed again and had turned an orange or tangerine colour. He appeared, to say the least, conspicuous.

Hanratty was first brought back to London and put on an identification parade before four supporting witnesses. The petrol-pump attendant who had sold petrol to Michael Gregsten failed to pick out Hanratty as the back seat passenger in the Morris Minor, which was perhaps not surprising. James Trower picked out Hanratty as the driver of the Morris Minor which had ground its gears as it passed him but he had only had the briefest glimpse of the driver on that occasion. He later added that he had only seen the driver for two or three seconds and that for much of that time he saw only the back of his head as he drove away. Mr Skillett, involved in the exchange of unpleasantries at the roundabout, identified the driver as Hanratty. His passenger, Mr Blackhall, who had had a fuller view of the driver, did not think it was Hanratty and picked out another man on the parade. He later said that he would have picked out Alphon as the driver of the Morris Minor.

With two positive and two negative witnesses, the identification of Hanratty as the suspect seemed finely balanced. A further problem was Hanratty's changed appearance. It might seem that as a disguise it would help him. Yet in any line of men he now stood out, as his counsel described it, 'like a carrot in a bunch of bananas'.

On the following day, 14 October, the crucial identification parade was held before Valerie Storie at Stoke Mandeville Hospital. It was not revealed until thirty years later that some time previously she had said of her assailant to Superintendent Acott, 'My memory of this man's face is fading.' After almost two months, how could it be otherwise?

The other members of the identification parade were men from an RAF station near Aylesbury. In the nature of things, they were well-groomed and of a regulation appearance. Hanratty stood among them with his mop of orange hair. He was also reported to be showing a very visible and understandable anxiety. Those who saw him recalled him as the tensest looking person they had ever seen. After all, he knew that the next few minutes would probably decide whether he lived or died and that he stood out conspicuously from all the other men.

Identification parades seldom last more than two or three minutes before each witness. According to those present, it took Valerie Storie fifteen minutes or so. She asked each man to say, 'Be quiet, will you? I am thinking.' In the end she picked out Hanratty during the last minute of the parade. That it took her a long time to decide did not necessarily mean that she was uncertain, and she never afterwards wavered in her assertion that Hanratty was the murderer of Michael Gregsten. That evening, he was charged with the crime.

4

With Valerie Storie's identification, there was now a strong case against Hanratty. All the same, he seemed an unlikely type of criminal to be wandering about at dusk in rural Buckinghamshire with a gun in his hand – looking for what? He was a small-time north London burglar and a car thief with no record of violence or sexual offences, and he had never been known to use or possess a gun. But, then, if he was the man who abducted Valerie Storie and Michael Gregsten, his past non-violence counted for nothing. There was, after all, always a first time for such things. If Valerie Storie's identification was questioned, it could only be because she never saw the murderer except in darkness or fleetingly by car head-lights, and because her memory of his face had faded over a period of seven weeks. As for his voice, Hanratty certainly said 'finking', rather than 'thinking', but so did thousands of other Londoners. Among those thousands, according to some who knew him, was Peter Alphon.

Was Hanratty the man? Valerie Storie was confident, but the other witnesses who identified him might be open to honest doubt. James Trower saw the driver of a car passing him at thirty feet per second. How much would he have seen through a car window and how well would the image lodge in his memory when he had no reason to think it of importance? Mr Skillett identified the driver as Hanratty but his passenger Mr Blackhall, who was closer and had a fuller view, picked out another man.

It was soon pointed out that if Hanratty was the A6 murderer, he was uncharacteristically inept in starting and driving the Morris Minor, perhaps the most common car on the roads of Britain at the time and a very easy vehicle to drive. Michael Sherrard QC, Hanratty's counsel, summed up this doubt, describing how Valerie Storie had to assist the gunman. 'Twice she started the car for him. Twice she had to explain how the gears of a Morris Minor worked, and where the reversing light was and where the lights were and so on. Does that sound like a car thief? Does that sound like somebody who runs around with a Jaguar motor-car key in his pocket? Does that sound like somebody who is an experienced car thief? I suggest that it does not.' Nor did it sound like a man who six weeks later knew how to get a key made within minutes for a Jaguar Mark 7 and drive it at once from London to Manchester in the middle of the night.

There was, however, one man who was not a driver and who might very well have had difficulty starting the Morris Minor at Deadman's Hill and changing gear as he passed Mr Trower. Peter Alphon was not a competent driver and was later to confess unavailingly to the A6 murder.

If such difficulties in driving a car suggested that Hanratty was not the man, some of the things he said to Michael Gregsten and Valerie Storie suggested the contrary. He claimed he was on the run and, indeed, Hanratty was then wanted for housebreaking, having left his fingerprints on the window ledge of a house he had burgled. The man also said that he had done sentences of corrective training and preventive detention, in the former case having 'done the lot', without remission. This was true of Hanratty, though someone might have said it on his behalf. The killer had said that his two victims could call him 'Jim'. Why on earth would he have given them his real name, especially when there was no need for him to give them any name at all? Was someone else trying to sound like Hanratty?

Other fragments of the conversation hardly sounded like Hanratty. The gunman seemed to be an habitué of the Bear Hotel at Maidenhead, which Hanratty had little opportunity to be and might not have chosen to be. Once again this raised the question of what a petty criminal and car thief like Hanratty would have been doing, wandering on foot in rural Buckinghamshire without transport but with a loaded revolver in his hand.

In another area of evidence, James Hanratty, in custody, volunteered to give samples so that forensic tests could be carried out. The tests showed nothing to link him with the crime and the car. Perhaps the only shadow of suspicion in that respect was that the man who raped Valerie Storie belonged to blood group C. Hanratty certainly belonged to that group but, then, so did forty-seven per cent of the population. As for his fingerprints, he was wearing gloves, as Valerie Storie recalled. Yet there was a good deal of blood in the car and it might seem surprising that not a drop of it had stained Hanratty's clothes or had been noticed as doing so. For the rest, not a single hair nor a fibre linked him to the car.

A point of contention was a dark suit belonging to Hanratty, the jacket of which was missing by the time he was arrested. The murderer had, of course, been described as wearing a dark lounge suit. The prosecution naturally suggested that Hanratty had worn the suit on the night of the murder and disposed of the jacket for fear that it might yield bloodstains or fibres linking him to his victims. But why did he not dispose of the trousers and waistcoat as well? How could he be sure that they did not have fibres or bloodstains on them? Hanratty insisted that he had torn the jacket while breaking into a house in Stanmore. He had stolen another jacket from the house, cut up his own and thrown it away. The prosecution naturally said that there was no such theft and the police confirmed that no jacket had been reported stolen in the course of any robbery in the area Hanratty had named. It was left largely to defence investigators to prove them wrong. The house in Stanmore was identified and it was confirmed that a jacket had been stolen from its owner during the course of the robbery which Hanratty described.

The case against Hanratty depended principally on identification and information received. The quality of some of that evidence was suspect. William Nudds, who gave the police three differing accounts of Hanratty and Alphon at the Vienna Hotel, had done time in prison for fraud and was well-known in the underworld as a police informer, by the name of 'The Squealer'. He was also to be dismissed as assistant manager of the Vienna Hotel and was to be sent to prison for fraud the following year. In his first statement, he recalled Alphon booking in at the hotel at 11.30 p.m. on 22 August, a cast-iron alibi for the A6 murder. Helpfully, he also told the police that Hanratty had asked him where to get a 36 bus. Mr Nudds then made a second statement saying that he had mistaken the times in his first account. Alphon's movements were unaccounted for between midday on 22 August until he was seen in his bedroom at about 10 a.m. the following morning. Alphon had had ample opportunity to commit the A6 crime and get back to the hotel, so far as Nudds could tell. Moreover, early on 22 August, Alphon had occupied Room 24, where the two cartridge cases had been found, before Room 6 was available.

But Mr Nudds then came forward a third time to say that his first statement, giving Alphon an alibi, was correct after all. His explanation for the second statement was almost engagingly frank. 'I decided that I could do myself a good turn by helping the police in an important job by giving them the information they appeared to want.'

The sensible course would have been to trust nothing that Mr Nudds said. Yet he was not the only person who was improbably helpful to the police. Hanratty's Soho friend Charles France was a petty criminal who came forward after the discovery of the gun on the 36A bus to say that the wanted man had told him the back seat on the upper deck was a good hiding place. There was, of course, no independent or trustworthy evidence to establish whether Hanratty had said any such thing. And why hide the gun in a place where he would never find it again but the police or the transport authorities might? If he wanted to be rid of it, why not just drop it in the river?

There was no doubt that the cartridge cases from the murder weapon had been found in Room 24 of the Vienna Hotel, but who had left them there? If it was Hanratty, he must have left them there before the murder, not after it. He had booked out of the Vienna Hotel twelve hours before the abduction. Where and when had the bullets belonging to the two cartridge cases been fired? Peter Alphon, who would have had relatively easy access to the unoccupied room even if he was not sleeping in it, could have left the cartridge cases there after the murder. As for the discovery of the gun, the 36A bus went along the Harrow Road, at the end of Sutherland Avenue, where the Vienna Hotel was situated. The gun was presumably left under the back seat on 23 August. Hanratty could have left it there. So could Alphon or anyone who was in the Vienna Hotel on the morning of 23 August, a very short distance from the bus route.

Perhaps the most dubious of all the prosecution witnesses was Roy Langdale, awaiting sentence in Brixton prison for forgery while Hanratty was on remand there. Langdale told the police that Hanratty had confessed to being the A6 murderer while they were in the exercise yard of the prison together. Hanratty was 'sex mad', according to Langdale, and confided that he still became sexually excited when he thought of how he had committed rape at Deadman's Hill. The chance of raping the young woman once he had got her male companion out of the way was what had inspired him to approach them in the Buckinghamshire field.

With every word that Langdale spoke, however, an impartial observer might recall the man's long criminal history and the fact that he had everything to gain by ingratiating himself with the police before he was sentenced to years of imprisonment for his forgery conviction. 'He has been very helpful to us on occasion,' was the testimonial given him. Langdale judged the situation well. When he came up for sentence, he did not go to prison at all. But was his story true? According to other prisoners, Hanratty and Langdale had virtually no contact with one another in Brixton, where Hanratty consistently affirmed his innocence. In the world where Hanratty moved, Langdale was generally known as an informer. Even if he had the opportunity, would Hanratty have been such a fool as to confide in a man with that reputation?

5

Discarding those witnesses who could not be relied upon, setting aside doubts and inconsistencies, there was still a case against Hanratty. Almost all of its strength appeared in the quiet heroic figure of Valerie Storie. She was honest, supremely courageous, and resourceful. If a jury believed her, that would be the end of the argument. No one could contradict her version of events because no one else was there. Hanratty's only hope lay in establishing an alibi. When the trial began, he was still insisting that he had been in Liverpool on the night of 22 August. He had gone there to sell stolen goods and had met several men who were criminal associates. They refused to implicate themselves in the murder case and would not confirm his alibi. That being so, he refused to name them. They would do his case nothing but harm.

It was after the trial began that Hanratty produced the defence which might have saved him. He left it very late and by varying the story he had told Superintendent Acott he sounded evasive, if not dishonest. The trial at Bedford Shire Hall in January 1962 was in its second week when he instructed his defence team to run what became known as 'The Rhyl Alibi'.

According to this, Hanratty had gone to Liverpool from London on the morning of 22 August, some twelve hours before the abduction, as he told Superintendent Acott. But he had not, after all, spent the night there. He had travelled along the North Wales coast to Rhyl and had been there, two hundred miles away from Deadman's Hill, when Michael Gregsten was murdered. This defence was left desperately late but, if it worked, it was a complete answer to the charge.

To make matters worse, however, Hanratty could not remember many details of his visit to Rhyl, not even the name of the street in which he had found bed and breakfast. He was certain only that he had slept in a room at the top of a boarding house with a green bath in it and that it was within earshot of the railway line. With the trial already proceeding, investigators on behalf of the defence set out for Rhyl.

Up to this point, the only evidence to support Hanratty's alibi was slight. He claimed that he had been in Liverpool on 22 August, the day of the crime, and had gone into a sweetshop in Scotland Road late that afternoon to ask the way. Mrs Olive Dinwoodie served in the shop on 21 and 22 August, not on any day after that. She identified Hanratty, from a photograph shown her by the police, as having come into the shop. She was not sure which day it had been but eventually decided it was 21 August because her grand-daughter was helping her. It proved that her grand-daughter had also been in the shop for half an hour or so on 22 August at the time when Hanratty claimed to have gone in. Both Charles France and his daughter Carol gave evidence that Hanratty was in London on 21 August, a date which was verified by a dentist who had taken out a tooth for Carol France that day, when Hanratty had seen her recuperating on a sofa from the extraction.

It was too little and almost too late. However, the investigators in Rhyl discovered the boarding-house, Ingledene in Kinmel Street. It was within earshot of the railway line. At the top of the house was a room with a green bath. When Ingledene was full, that top room was used as an extra bedroom. Mrs Grace Jones, the owner of Ingledene, identified Hanratty from a photograph as having stayed in the house during the week of 19 to 26 August. He had stayed for two nights. Even if Mrs Dinwoodie had seen him in Liverpool on 21, rather than 22 August, and he had already been on his way to Rhyl, he could not be the A6 murderer.

The evidence of Mrs Jones became the foundation of Hanratty's defence. Yet his fate was to be decided not simply by what was true but by what could be proved in court. Much of this depended on the quality of those presenting the evidence – the witnesses. The Crown had produced a good deal of very unimpressive evidence from informers or criminals. But in Valerie Storie they had a first-class witness.

Though it was not relevant to the issue of Hanratty's guilt, no one could see the young woman without instinctive sympathy and without admiration for her courage and presence of mind.

Quite apart from that, Miss Storie alone had seen the murderer at the time of the killing. She had picked out James Hanratty on the identification parade and never afterwards wavered in her assertion that he was the killer. Under examination and cross-examination, she stuck to her version of events. Because she was alone with the assailant, there could be no corroboration. However, Mr Trower and Mr Skillett both identified Hanratty as the man they had seen driving the Morris Minor a few hours after the murder. A jury would surely regard that as corroboration enough.

Hanratty gave a reasonably good account of himself in the witness box, though some observers thought he was 'cocky' rather than confident. He wrote to his parents afterwards that he had answered every question 'truthfully and correctly'. It was certainly an impression that he strove to give. Though he made no bones about his criminal record, he held his ground much of the time. On occasion he seemed to get the better of his cross-examiner. When Graham Swanwick QC suggested that he was a gunman, 'a stick-up' man, rather than a burglar and that was why he had dyed his hair, Hanratty pointed out that a stick-up man would wear a mask and not bother about the colour of his hair.

But the alibi was everything to the defence. As a witness, Mrs Grace Jones was not in her first youth and was no match for Valerie Storie. She was brought from Rhyl and propelled into the assize court with very little warning. She knew nothing about the rules governing legal proceedings. Her first error was in quite innocently discussing the case with another witness from Rhyl outside the courtroom. This led to her being reprimanded before the court by the judge. She gave evidence that she recognized Hanratty, from the photograph and in court, as the man who had stayed two nights at her guest house in the week of 19-26 August, almost certainly on 22 August. The house had been full and he had been put in the top room, which had a green bath but was used as an extra bedroom. Her daughter was later to add that other guests who were produced as Crown witnesses to say they had never seen him were quite right. They would not necessarily have seen him. Because the boarding house was full, there was no room for him in the five-table dining room at breakfast. He had his breakfast in the family's own living room at the back of the house.

Mrs Jones did not do well under cross-examination. She had not kept a complete register of her guests, especially of those who were rather casually accommodated. Hanratty's presence at the guest-house was vouched for only by her memory and not by any entry in the register, which the Crown had appropriated. At one point, Mr Swanwick suggested that she had only appeared as a witness in order to get publicity for her house.

Though there were other witnesses who might have helped to place Hanratty in Rhyl, they were not called by the defence, after the fate of Mrs Jones. Two of them were reasonably sure they had seen him on the evening of 22 August but thought his hair was different. Of course, his hair was then dark brown, as they recalled. Mr Christopher Larman made a statement that he had seen Hanratty in Rhyl at about 7.30 p.m. Like the others, he remembered that Hanratty was looking for somewhere to stay and he was positive as to the identity of the man and the date. Mr Michael Da Costa had seen a man he identified as Hanratty at Euston Station on the morning of 22 August, presumably on his way to Liverpool. One problem was that the Rhyl witnesses would have put Hanratty in the town at about 7.30 p.m., whereas Hanratty recalled his bus arriving there as it was getting dark, which would have been about an hour later.

The question of the alibi was to haunt the case long after Hanratty's execution. At the time of his trial, however, there were obvious difficulties over the supporting evidence. The witnesses were not approached until five months after the event. They could not be shown Hanratty but only a photograph of him. On this basis, they were sometimes no more than reasonably certain that Hanratty was the young man they had seen. In all honesty, they could not always say they were certain beyond question. But Mr Larman, who was otherwise unknown to Hanratty, had no hesitation in identifying him. Nor did Mr Da Costa.

Many points about the alibi made by the prosecution were later answered, but they were not answered at the trial.

Hanratty only remembered two tables in the room where he had breakfast. There were five tables in the dining-room. But, as an extra guest, he had breakfast in the family room. It contained two tables. There was a betting-shop in the street, three doors away, with an illuminated sign of a jockey with a whip. How could he not remember that? It was later established that the illuminated sign had not been there on 22 August, though it was in place by the time of the trial.

As the hearing at Bedfordshire Assizes drew to its close on 17 February 1962, it had been the longest murder trial in English legal history. At 11.20 a.m., Mr Justice Gorman sent the jurors to consider their verdict. 'You have now upon you the duty, in accordance with the oath which you have taken, upon the evidence given in this court, to say whether the prosecution have proved, so that you are sure, that James Hanratty murdered by shooting Michael John Gregsten.'

The jury retired and the hours passed. Louis Blom-Cooper QC was present at the trial. He wrote afterwards that, 'far into the afternoon the feeling of an informed onlooker was increasingly that on the evidence before the court a jury should not convict Hanratty of the crime with which he was charged. The element of doubt persisted, and as the hours flickered by, the thought of an acquittal gathered of its own momentum.'

At 5.45 p.m. on that Saturday evening, after almost six and a half hours, it was murmured that the jury was coming back. The courtroom filled, Hanratty was brought up from the cells and the judge took his place. The foreman of the jury stood up. But it was not a verdict. The jurors wanted to know whether they must judge the case on reasonable doubt or be certain and sure of the prisoner's guilt. And where there was circumstantial evidence, could it be evidence against the accused if there were other possible explanations? It sounded as if the jurors might be leaning towards an acquittal.

Mr Justice Gorman told them that they must be able to exclude all doubt, except such as was unreasonable. Where circumstantial evidence existed, it must point 'inevitably' to the accused, or else it was not evidence against him. The jury retired again. An hour and a half later, they came back. But still there was no verdict. They asked for some refreshment. The strain of the delay showed principally in Hanratty's face, but also in those of the judge and the onlookers. Mr Justice

Gorman ordered that tea and sandwiches should be provided. The jurors retired again. Two more hours passed. Then at 9.10 p.m., after almost ten hours of deliberation, the jury returned and gave a verdict of guilty. The death penalty was mandatory. Hanratty seemed to sag forward against the dock-rail and mumbled his innocence semi-coherently before saying that he would appeal. Some of those present reported that the judge looked shocked by the verdict. He hesitated before speaking the familiar words by which James Hanratty was sentenced to death.

6

In the years that followed, the verdict bred doubt and dissension. There was an appeal, based upon the alleged misdirection of the jury by the trial judge in his summing-up. It failed. The further evidence of the Rhyl alibi was kept for submission to the Home Secretary, R.A. Butler, in support of the petition for a reprieve, a petition signed by 90,000 people. Two more witnesses were found who both offered evidence about a man bearing a strong resemblance to Peter Alphon who had frequented the Old Station Inn at Taplow and had been seen in Marsh Lane the previous summer. The Old Station Inn was the pub from which Michael Gregsten and Valerie Storie had set out on the night of the murder. Marsh Lane bordered the cornfield where the gunman had appeared in the dusk. The police had been informed about the man at the time of the murder but had apparently done nothing further. The Marsh Lane witness later alleged that he had the man's hand-print on his car but that the policeman who examined it said, 'It's a bad night for fingerprints.' He wiped it off and was subsequently discovered to have left the force. If true, the story was a chill echo of Hanratty's comment as he waited to be hanged, 'It's surprising what the law can do to an innocent man.'

If Hanratty was innocent, then he was certainly not very bright. If the Rhyl alibi meant anything at all, why did he not give it to his defenders at the start? Those who might have supported his story would have been asked about him in October or November, when they would have been better able to remember, rather than three months later. The petty thieves whom he was going to pay to tell the 'truth' about his Liverpool visit, as he told Superintendent Acott, would scarcely have lasted two minutes under skilful cross-examination.

The alibi was weakened by the way in which it appeared to be sprung on the jury. Why that jury convicted Hanratty we shall never know. Self-evidently, they did not believe the Rhyl alibi. Though they ought not to have been swayed by personal dislike of Hanratty in the witness-box, it has to be said that he did not reveal himself to them as an amiable young man. By his own account, he felt nothing for the people he robbed. He had no misgivings over the distress they felt when he stole from them those things which held more than material value for them. If he cared so little about the distress of others, was he really just 'a bit of a crook' with no real harm in him? Did he care so little in the end that he would put two bullets into a man without much compunction? Such thoughts are not evidence, but they may not be without influence. With the case so finely balanced on the evidence, the impression made by the accused surely counted for more than it might otherwise have done.

None of the new post-trial evidence, true or not, was to save Hanratty. No reprieve was granted. Awaiting execution in Bedford Prison, he wrote to his parents and other members of his family. He showed great courage, even when all hope was gone, and insisted on his innocence, even when that insistence would do him no further good. 'You know I wouldn't do a thing like that,' he wrote to his mother of the A6 murder. When the reprieve was refused on 2 April 1962 and he was to be executed two days later, Hanratty wrote to his father, 'The only way I can pay my respect to you and the family is to show what kind of man I really am, though I am about to take the punishment for someone else's crime, I will face it like a man, and show both courage and strength, and try to make you proud of your son.'

Two Catholic priests attended Hanratty and revealed that to the moment of his death he maintained his innocence of the crime. Father John Hughes was so convinced of his charge's innocence and so disturbed about the impending miscarriage of justice that he made his misgivings public before the execution. Despite this, the law took its course. On the morning of 4 April 1962, James Hanratty was hanged in

Bedford Prison. It is said that he died with the courage which he had promised his parents he would show.

One curiosity of the case was not revealed in the press until after the trial. On 31 August 1961, eight days after the murder of Michael Gregsten, his widow Janet saw a man going into a dry cleaner's shop in Swiss Cottage. She knew at once and intuitively that this man with the blue staring eyes was her husband's murderer. 'That's the man the police are looking for,' Mrs Gregsten said. She had no evident reason for thinking this, especially since the police had been looking for a man with brown deep-set eyes, though the description was changed later that day.

It was discovered from the dry cleaner's that the man's name was J. Ryan. Next day he was seen again, going into a florist's shop nearby. The flowers he purchased were to be sent to Mrs Hanratty. 'J. Ryan' was, of course, the pseudonym used by James Hanratty. By 31 August the police had made no statement about Hanratty. Alphon was still the name linked to the investigation. Yet Mrs Gregsten, by a chance in a million, had seen James Hanratty and pointed him out as the A6 killer. Though the police were told, it was still Alphon who held their interest for three more weeks.

But other and later events cast further doubt on Hanratty's guilt. Two days after his appeal was dismissed, the prosecution witness Charles 'Dixie' France went to a bed-sit in London and gassed himself. Peter Alphon, the man who attracted so much suspicion, was acquitted of the charge of assault and attempted rape against Mrs Meike Dalal. As Jean Justice and others tried to establish the truth of the A6 murder, Alphon remained coy, saying only that Hanratty was 'expendable'. Five years later in Paris, on 12 May 1967, with the press in attendance at the Hôtel du Louvre, Peter Alphon made a detailed confession to the A6 murder. He claimed that he had been paid money to separate Michael Gregsten and Valerie Storie. The gun had been procured for him by Charles 'Dixie' France. It was France who had then framed Hanratty by hiding the gun on the 36A bus and by leaving two cartridge cases in Room 24 of the Vienna Hotel.

Alphon withdrew this confession subsequently and then confessed again. Two official inquiries did nothing to alter Hanratty's case. Was the man who called himself 'a bit of a crook', but who 'would not harm a mouse', hanged in error?

It now seems beyond proof or disproof. The one thing certain is that a jury with all the evidence available, as opposed to what was heard at the trial, would surely have acquitted James Hanratty on the basis of a reasonable doubt and would not have taken ten hours to do so.

7 How Can They Be So Sure?

1

No one has been hanged in England since the abolition of capital punishment for murder in 1964. Treason, however, remains a capital offence and the gallows at Wandsworth prison have been preserved. They are tested once a month with a sandbag on the end of the rope, as an academic exercise.

Since the abolition of the death penalty, the number of cases in which men and women have been shown to be wrongly convicted of murder has risen sharply, according to subsequent findings of the Court of Criminal Appeal. There are two commonsense explanations for this. If a man is hanged, any campaign to prove his innocence is purely a matter of principle. He is dead and nothing will bring him back. Unless strongly motivated and supported, protest dwindles away. If the man is in prison for life, his best years passing in a punishment for something he did not do, his release is a practical aim.

In the second place, the hanging of a man may remove the chief witness to any injustice done him. If there are allegations of police coercion or malpractice, the only surviving witnesses may be those with most to hide.

The 1990s have seen a crop of cases in which those who have served years in prison have belatedly been found innocent. Arguments in favour of capital punishment often cite terrorism, child-murder or sexually motivated killing as crimes where hanging is the answer. Yet some of the most blatant miscarriages of justice have been in precisely those areas. Again, the reasons are not far to seek. There is great pressure on the police to bring to justice those responsible for

crimes which, naturally, rouse public anger. Where there is a
likely suspect the pressure, within and without the system, is
increased. A failure to get a conviction may be seen as a
defeat. In that lies the danger.

The consequences were demonstrated in the cases of the
Birmingham Six and the Guildford Four. The arrest of the
Guildford Four followed the bombings of two pubs in the
town during October 1974. They were assumed to be the
work of an IRA 'active service' unit planted in London.
Belfast-born Gerry Conlon later alleged that, having been
arrested in his native city, he was brought to London, beaten
up by police officers and forced to sign a confession. The
moment when he gave in was, he said, when one of the
officers told him that unless he signed the confession, an
accident would be 'arranged' for his mother.

The four defendants were convicted, though they retracted
their confessions. The Court of Criminal Appeal dismissed
their cases. Had capital punishment still existed, there seems
no doubt that they would have been hanged.

In the year after the four began their life sentences, the IRA
unit which had in reality caused the explosions was caught in
the Balcombe Street siege. The members confessed that they,
not the Guildford Four, were responsible for the pub
bombings. The Court of Criminal Appeal refused to accept
this as new evidence.

As early as the time of the trial, secret Scotland Yard
reports suggested that these four people had nothing to do
with the bombings or the IRA. Indeed, they had alibi
witnesses, including one, in Conlon's case, who had been
interviewed by the police but not called to give evidence. By
1989 the evidence against these four convictions was
embarrassingly plain. The Home Secretary ordered the
Devon and Cornwall Constabulary to undertake an inquiry
into the original investigation of the case. The result of the
inquiry left Douglas Hurd with no choice but to refer the case
back to the court of Criminal Appeal. At the hearing, the
Crown withdrew all charges against the accused. The
Guildford Four emerged from prison, having lost fifteen
years of their lives. Had the hangman still been in business,
they would almost certainly have lost their lives outright.

A month after the deaths and injuries at Guildford, a far
worse outrage occurred in Birmingham, where twenty-one

people were killed and sixty-two injured as bombs exploded in the Tavern in the Town and the Mulberry Bush. Within hours, the West Midlands police had arrested six men travelling to Liverpool by train, on their way to the funeral of an IRA bomber in Ulster. There was no doubt of their allegiance and two of them appeared to have traces of nitro-glycerine on their hands. The six were sentenced to life imprisonment by virtue of the scientific evidence and their confessions, obtained by means that were later to be the subject of controversy.

By 1990, in the wake of the successful campaign of the Guildford Four, there were greater misgivings in the Birmingham case. More scrupulous examination of the scientific evidence showed that the substance on the men's hands might have been a number of compounds other than nitro-glycerine, including household soap. An investigation of police notebooks suggested irregularities in the original notes of the interviews and confessions. There could only be one outcome. Six men who would have been hanged in 1974 or 1975, had capital punishment still been in use, walked free from the Court of Appeal in 1991.

In a quite different case, Stefan Kiszko would surely have gone to the gallows in 1975 for the brutal murder of an eleven-year-old schoolgirl, Lesley Molseed. The child had been taken, driven to the moors near Rochdale, dragged from the car, sexually assaulted and stabbed to death. She had been abducted while running an errand for her mother.

Stefan Kiszko, twenty-four years old, lived with his mother in Rochdale. He was a rather reclusive clerk, quiet and gentle, not of high intelligence but no one's idea of a sex-killer. There was surprise when it was announced that the police had arrested him and charged him with the murder of Lesley Molseed.

Why had Kiszko, of all people, been arrested? It was revealed that a number of local girls had gone to the police in the previous few weeks and complained that Stefan Kiszko had indecently exposed himself to them. He was, therefore, on the list of suspects for the murder. The girls later admitted that Stefan Kiszko had never exposed himself to them, nor had he ever behaved with the least impropriety. They had made the stories up because they thought he was 'stupid' and they resented him for this. It was what they called a

'lark', thinking it would be good fun to give him a fright
when the police called round to interview him. They would
then, presumably, have had to perjure themselves to
maintain their stories, or else be found out. Apparently, they
lacked the wit to see that far ahead.

With a local 'flasher' in custody, the Rochdale police went
to work. Stefan Kiszko was not a man of high IQ and during
two days of interrogation by Detective Superintendent Jack
Dibb of the Yorkshire police he found himself well out of
his depth. He needed the presence of a solicitor, but was not
yet given access to one. In the end, Kiszko made a
confession. Or rather, by his own account, the policeman
wrote the confession and he signed it. Why did he sign it?
After two days alone with his interrogators, 'I was scared,' he
said.

Stefan Kiszko's trial involved people who were soon to be
important public men. His counsel, David Waddington QC,
was a future Conservative Home Secretary. His prosecutor,
Peter Taylor QC, would one day be Lord Chief Justice. There
was no conclusive evidence against Kiszko except his
confession, which he now withdrew as having been made
under duress. There were fibres on Lesley Molseed's clothes
that could have come from a carpet in the Kiszko home, as
they could have come from thousands of other homes in the
area. His alibi was that he and his mother had gone with his
aunt to put flowers on his father's grave. No one believed
him. He was sentenced to life imprisonment when the jury
convicted him by a ten-to-two majority.

Mrs Kiszko never lost faith in her son's innocence. Had it
not been for the false accusations of indecent exposure, he
would probably never even have been regarded as a suspect
for the murder. Mrs Kiszko herself found little support until
1985. At length it was forensically established that semen on
the victim's clothes could not have come from Kiszko. Quite
simply, he was infertile and the assailant was not.

There was other evidence to suggest, from the very start,
that Kiszko could not be the killer. Given the multiple stab
wounds from which the girl had died, the complete absence
of blood on his clothing or in the car which he drove might
have caused some doubt. It was suggested that all the blood
had gone into the cavities of the body and none had come
out. But there was, in truth, no case against him. However,

he was refused leave to appeal and would no doubt have gone to the gallows as a child murderer, had hanging still prevailed. He went to prison at twenty-four and was released as a man of forty in 1992, when his innocence had been established. A year later, he was dead. True, he had not been hanged. Yet the law had taken all but this year of life from an innocent man.

The same year in which Kiszko was set free also saw the release of the Darvell brothers, sentenced to life imprisonment in 1986 for the murder of Sandra Phillips, a sex-shop manageress in Swansea. Not only had the brothers been convicted but their appeal had subsequently been heard and dismissed by the Court of Criminal Appeal. Twenty-two years earlier, nothing but a reprieve by the Home Secretary would have stood between them and the gallows. In the case of such a brutal rape and murder, they would surely have been prime candidates for judicial retribution. Yet the manner in which the case against them had been built up was what Chief Constable Robert Lawrence called, after their release, 'a cause of great concern'. An inquiry into the police conduct of the case was ordered. Once again, it was to be undertaken by the Devon and Cornwall Constabulary.

The abolition of hanging, the availability of those convicted as witnesses, makes it easier for us to understand just how murder investigations may go wrong. It is plainer to see how, in the past, men and women might be hanged in error. Between 1989 and 1992, forty people were freed by the Court of Criminal Appeal after failures of police and scientific evidence, uncorroborated confessions, and non-disclosure of material to defence lawyers. The most instructive case was yet to come, showing clearly the mechanics of injustice in a murder trial, which would once have put a noose round the neck of each plausible suspect.

2

The locale of the crime was almost poetic. Traditionally, there are few place-names to conjure up a more potent image of murder, vice, squalor or waterfront violence and racial mixing than Cardiff's dockland of 'Tiger Bay'. Mary Kelly, the last prostitute murdered by Jack the Ripper, began her career on its pavements. Policemen never patrolled alone. Pimping and theft went side by side with a close sense of community and loyalty in the streets of little houses. Large areas of that community were extended families, the stevedores and stokers, donkeymen and dredger crews of a great port. Those whose money and possessions went the way of the pimps and thieves were usually outsiders.

Tiger Bay is now more blandly known as Butetown, Cardiff's dockland. It is divided from much of the city to the north by the London to South Wales railway line, on the east by the dock basins, and on the west by the River Taff, running between long sloping banks of mud. To the south, Cardiff Bay is sheltered by the dock wall on one side and the marshland of the Taff and Ely estuaries on the other.

Since the end of the Second World War, the docks and the South Wales coal trade which supported them had been in decline. By contrast, in the 1980s, the centre of Cardiff had acquired an improbable air of chic. Tourists came to the Edwardian-Rococo buildings of the Civic Centre, where the National Museum of Wales housed a world-famous collection of impressionist paintings. Nearby, the Welsh National Opera had transformed the old variety hall of the New Theatre. Cardiff Castle remained a Pre-Raphaelite extravaganza, set in riverside parkland.

But the visitor who walked through the city, past the plate-glass display windows of department stores in the High Street and St Mary Street, moved into another and shabbier world. The roadway dipped down under the plate-iron railway bridge, carrying the lines from London and from the South Wales valleys into the central station. Beyond this bridge lay Tiger Bay, the central stem of Bute Street running straight for a mile to the dry docks and the pier head, from which P & A Campbell's paddle-steamers once served the Bristol Channel. The dock wall and Penarth Head enclosed a world of shining mud-flats and reeds at low tide.

On the east side, Bute Street was a drab railway wall, where one line branched down to the docks. This wall marked the frontier of an area where prostitutes, some as young as thirteen, solicited passing motorists. Many of the adolescents were runaways from assessment centres like Maes-yr-Eglwys near Pontypridd, where social services held girls remanded on criminal charges or beyond parental control. The world of under-age prostitution in Cardiff dockland was to be chillingly detailed in the trial of two men for the murder of Karen Price in 1991 – the case of 'The Body in the Carpet' (described in my 1993 book, *Dead Giveaway*).

On the other side of Bute Street lay streets of terraced housing with a mission church and corner pubs, dating from the port's Edwardian prosperity. Behind this ensemble rose the apartment blocks of new municipal housing. At the far end of Bute Street's mile was an area of banks and commercial premises, a quayside whose pier-head had by now fallen into the mud, a fine red-brick Customs House in imitation of Calais town hall. Mountstuart Square with its impressive Coal Exchange building was a reminder of better days.

At the centre of this commercial area, just short of the pier-head, Bute Street was crossed at the traffic lights by James Street, many of its drab pavement-front houses converted to shops or betting offices on the ground floor. By 1988, the house at 7 James Street was almost derelict above the Kingsport betting office at street level. Both the water and the electricity had been cut off in its first-floor flat.

On the evening of 14 February 1988, police were called to the first-floor flat. Sergeant Bisgood and Constable Prosser arrived at 9.17 p.m. In the room overlooking the street, there was a bed that had not been made up. On the bed was some money and an unused condom. Across the wall and the bed was an arc of dried bloodstains with further marks of blood below the window. There was also a palm print on the wall.

In the narrow space between the bed and the wall lay the body of a young white woman. Her name was Lynette White and she was twenty-one years old. She was known to the police from her convictions as a prostitute who worked the streets of Butetown, sometimes bringing men back to the room at £10 a time, sometimes going with them in their cars. Her death had resulted from a demented attack. She had been stabbed fifty-one times, many of these wounds having been made after death. Her throat had been cut more than once, almost to the spine, with such savagery that she was nearly decapitated.

Lynette White's body was fully clothed in jeans and jumper, white trainers and a blue denim jacket. There were marks of blood on the legs of her jeans. Professor Bernard

Knight, of the Institute of Pathology at Cardiff's Royal Infirmary, arrived at 3.10 a.m. Lynette White had died in the small hours of the previous morning. Professor Knight reported that 'the major wound on the body was a massive cut throat which extended from below the right ear diagonally downwards across the front of the neck and around the left side where it ended beneath the angle of the jaw.'

It seemed likely that she had died between 1 a.m. and 2 a.m. that Sunday morning. Within a few hours of the discovery of her body, her twenty-two-year-old boy-friend Stephen Miller went to Butetown police station. He made a statement and was eliminated from the inquiry. Lynette had supported his £60 a day drink and drugs habit, but she had gone missing from the flat they shared at the beginning of February and it was impossible to say what she had been doing since. Two witnesses were able to say that Miller had been at the Casablanca Club the night before. One had been with him between about 11 p.m. and 3 a.m., the other at 1.30 a.m. precisely. According to his later account, the police asked Miller to go back on the street and talk to anyone who had known Lynette White in the hope of adding to their information. He said that he did so but that no one knew anything.

It was later to be of importance in the case that Miller was black, that his IQ was 74 (one point above subnormal) that he had a mental age of eleven and a reading age of eight.

Superintendent John Williams, a veteran of successful South Wales murder inquiries, was in charge of the case. He was able to establish from Barbara Leith and another eye-witness that at the time of the murder a white man was seen outside the flat where Lynette White's body was found. The flat was not hers, apparently, but belonged to another Butetown prostitute, Leanne Vilday, who was not using it at the time. The white man outside the flat was described as being thirty-five to forty years old, between five feet eight inches and six feet tall. He was distressed, crying, had cut himself, and had blood on his hands.

At that point, however, the investigation reached a dead-end. In March 1988, the month after the murder, John Williams appealed for information through the BBC's *Crimewatch* programme. Its presenter, Nick Ross, suggested to him that the man seen outside the flat must be 'the prime suspect'. John Williams agreed. 'That is right. He certainly is a person we must speak to at this time. And we must remember that this man was bleeding himself, he's cut himself, he's also got blood on him from the deceased.'

A white man, referred to in subsequent proceedings as Mr X, was regarded by the South Wales Intelligence Bureau as the most likely suspect after two months of investigation. He was a man of below average intelligence who had twice been a patient in a psychiatric hospital. He had convictions for sexual offences. More to the point, he had been one of Lynette White's clients. He associated with another man who was staying in the flat above the room in which Lynette was murdered, on the night she had been killed. His blood group, which was so rare that it was probably shared by only twenty or thirty other men in the city, matched that of a bloodstain found on the leg of Lynette White's jeans. An attempt to match his blood with the stain by DNA testing failed, not because there was no match but because the sample on the jeans was apparently not adequate. Since the DNA test produced nothing, Mr X was kept under surveillance but was not yet charged. However, the press reported that 'a secret profile drawn up for police hunting the killer of prostitute Lynette White pointed the finger at a prime suspect labelled Mr X'.

Even when five men were tried for the murder of Lynette White, details of Mr X were withheld by the prosecution. It was not revealed that 'Mr X was a client of Lynette's, was regarded as a psychopath by his doctor, had convictions for rape and indecency, was prone to impulsive violence, and had previously been attacked by a woman with a machete during which he sustained serious injuries.' It was certainly not revealed that his rare blood group matched that on Lynette White's jeans.

3

Nine months after the murder, despite the psychological profile of the killer prepared for the police by Surrey University, it seemed that Mr X had been eliminated from the case. Then there occurred an extraordinary change in the evidence of three witnesses. One of them, Mark Gromek, had been the tenant of the flat above the murder room and his friend Paul Atkins had been staying with him on the night of 13–14 February. Mr Gromek now told the police, 'In this statement I would like to say exactly what took place. I am aware that I have not been truthful fully with you in the past'. For the first time in nine months and many statements, he described how the bell by the street door had rung at about 1.30 a.m. on 14 February. 'On the pavement there were four male persons. I know two of these persons to be Dullah, whose first name is Yusef, and the second to be Ronnie Actie. I know these persons from the North Star Club'. 'Dullah' was Yusef Abdullahi. The North Star was a Butetown club, rather like a prefabricated church hall in appearance. Mark Gromek claimed that he had seen the four men, none of them white, enter the house. He recognized two as Ronald Actie and Yusef Abdullahi. The four arrivals had gone up to Lynette White's room. Soon afterwards, there were shouts and screams. Paul Atkins went down to the first-floor flat to see what the noise was. He returned to say that a girl had been murdered.

On the far side of James Street, over two hundred feet from the room where the murder took place, two other young prostitutes, Leanne Vilday and Angela Psaila, occupied a flat. Both had been questioned about the murder. Leanne Vilday made twenty different statements and Angela Psaila eleven over the course of the investigation. If they told the truth in their new statements, then they had lied repeatedly in the earlier ones. They now made statements, describing how they had heard the screams. They ran across the street and entered the room. In this new version of events, eight men were engaged in the murder of Lynette White, though this number was reduced to five in further statements. Angela Psaila told the police that she had looked out of the window of the flat and seen a number of men outside the door of 7 James Street, including Tony Paris, Stephen Miller, and John Actie, as well as Ronnie Actie and Yusef Abdullahi, the two whom Mark Gromek placed there.

It was about 1.45 a.m., when Leanne Vilday and Angela Psaila heard screams coming from the flat at 7 James Street, which Leanne Vilday had lent to Lynette White. 'On the second floor I heard screaming and again looked from the window,' Leanne Vilday added. 'It was coming from the flat. We ran down the stairs and went across to the flat .... I went up the stairs first and Angela was behind me. I ran up the stairs and into the living room .... I ran into the living room, followed by Angela. When I got in there, I saw Lynette lying on the floor by the bed and by the far window.'

She alleged that Ronald Actie was standing by the door and Yusef Abdullahi just beyond him inside the room. Stephen Miller, Lynette's boyfriend, and Tony Paris from the nearby Casablanca Club were standing over Lynette White. Tony Paris was stabbing her in the chest. Lynette White was lying between the bed and the window. They could not see whether she was alive or dead. John Actie, Ronnie Actie's cousin, was handed the knife. He turned to Leanne Vilday, telling her to cut Lynette White's wrists, ensuring her complicity and silence.

'I cut through Lynette's right wrist.... I dropped the knife on the floor. Angela was screaming at them, yelling "You dirty bastards! She don't deserve killing...." It could have been John or Tony because they were standing by her. Steve said, "Take the knife, it's her turn now." John passed Angela the knife. Angela was told by John to cut the other wrist. He put the knife in her hand like he did mine. She then bent over and with John's help cut Lynette's other wrist. Stephen took the knife off Angela and told me to take the knife and cut Lynette's throat. He offered me the knife but I refused to take it....' Sometime during this, Paul Atkins came in from the upstairs flat, saw what had happened and went out again. One of the girls shouted, 'You fucking bastards!' and ran out of the room.

Such were the stories told to the police in November and December 1988. All three witnesses were known to them, Vilday and Psaila as prostitutes, Mark Gromek as a man who was on probation for shoplifting and had served a three-year sentence for attempted armed robbery. Of the five who were now arrested on suspicion of murdering Lynette White, Stephen Miller was known as a user of cocaine, Tony Paris had a conviction for shoplifting and Yusef Abdullahi a conviction for violence some years before. They were known to the police but not for any major crime. More to the point, they apparently had nothing in common with Mr X, certainly not their skin colour.

The five men denied having had anything to do with the murder of Lynette White. On the face of it, that seemed probable. None of their blood samples matched the blood in the stains found on the wall of the room and the legs of the girl's jeans. There was forensic evidence but none of it, not even a fingerprint or a hair, connected these five suspects with the murder.

The Actie cousins were to be acquitted. The other three men had alibis. Stephen Miller was placed in the Casablanca Club by two witnesses. Derek Ferron remembered that 'About 1.30 a.m. I went alone to the Casablanca Club. Stephen was standing in the Comet on his own. I spoke to him and he asked me for money. I gave him two pounds.' David Leonard Orton had gone to the club with Stephen Miller the previous evening. 'We stayed there till closing time. This was about 3 a.m. We were together all the time in the Casablanca. There was a show in there and we were playing pool in there. We kept ourselves to ourselves.' Stephen Miller had told the police that he went to the Casablanca Club 'at about 10.15 p.m.' and had not left before closing time.

Tony Paris was placed at the club by another witness, Paul Anthony Sinclair, who replied to police suggestions that Paris might have left the club, committed the murder and returned without being missed. 'My answer to that is no, he did not leave because he is needed all the time in his role as glass-collector and if he had left them there would have been a pile-up of dirty glasses.

Yusef Abdullahi, known familiarly as 'Dulla', or 'Dullah', had the best alibi of all. He had been working all night on a ship, the *Coral Sea*, in Barry Dock. He was eight miles away with no transport. A number of witnesses had seen him there. Was it possible that he could have got off the ship unseen, found transport, made his way to Cardiff, met up with the other men, gone to James Street and taken part in the killing of Lynette White, then made his way back to Barry and on to the ship again without his absence being noticed? Trains and buses had ceased running long before 1.30 a.m. Abdullahi had no transport of his own. He must somehow have got off the *Coral Sea*, called a taxi, been driven eight miles, much of it through built-up areas of Barry and western Cardiff, met his co-accused, gone to James Street and committed murder, all within about fifteen minutes. It was plainly absurd, if the witnesses were correct in their statements.

Apart from Mark Gromek, Leanne Vilday and Angela Psaila at the murder flat, only Ronald Williams claimed to have seen Abdullahi in Cardiff, at the North Star club in Butetown, though he later added that he could not be absolutely sure which night it was. Laurence Mann placed Ronald Williams himself on the *Coral Sea* that night, as the friend who had driven him home at 1.30 a.m. There was not a single witness, neither a ship's labourer nor a taxi-driver, to support the suggestion that Abdullahi could have got from Barry Dock to Cardiff. Thirteen witnesses supported his alibi in one way or another.

In many respects, Yusef Abdullahi was best placed to demolish the entire case, so far as it was supported by the two young prostitutes and Mark Gromek. Though his witnesses were asked about events nine months in the past, they were better able to place the night because it was a weekend, the night of Saturday night and Sunday morning. They could also place it because they were working on a particular ship, the *Coral Sea*, which happened to be in Barry Dock at the time. No doubt, the date also stuck more easily in the memory as the night on which a particularly savage murder had taken place in their relatively close-knit community of Butetown. A curiosity of this apparently anonymous prostitute-killing was how many people now allegedly involved in it seemed to have known one another beforehand. Indeed, the mother of Lynette White, Peggy Pesticcio, was the girlfriend of Alan Charlton, when Lynette was fourteen. Three months after the presumed killers of Lynette were convicted, Alan Charlton himself was to be sentenced to life imprisonment for the entirely unrelated 1981 murder of the juvenile prostitute Karen Price in the so-called 'Body in the Carpet' case.

Laurence Mann had reason to remember the events of Saturday and Sunday, 14–15 February 1988, the night on which Lynette White was murdered. He was thirty-three years old, trained as an actor but currently unemployed. His friend Ronald Williams told him that there was work on the *Coral Sea* and they went over in Mr Williams's car. Laurence Mann recalled, 'I worked straight through the day, not even stopping for a meal. I knew Yusef Abdullahi from the Custom House pub. I saw him for the first time on the Saturday night at approximately 11 p.m. He was standing on the poop deck next to the bridge with Peter McCarthy. I have never really spoken to him and don't have any real contact with him but I recognize him.... I remember that Ron and myself left the ship dead on 1.30 a.m. It had been drizzling with rain from about 11 p.m. but at 1.15 a.m. it began raining heavily. I remember I was sheltering under the bridge area with Brinley Samuel. I am definite about the time.' He saw Abdullahi as he left the ship. If that was so, it was quite impossible for Abdullahi to have been in Cardiff committing murder with the four other men fifteen minutes later.

The question raised by the police was whether Laurence Mann was remembering the correct night and the correct time. Faced with this query, he paid a visit to the Cardiff Weather Centre. 'I was so worried about the implications about my evidence that I went to the met office myself and checked which day it rained during that general period. The people at the met office told me that on Saturday 13 February 1988 it began raining at approximately 11 p.m. and continued until about 1.30 a.m. on Sunday 14 February 1988.'

Another witness was Brinley Samuel, a ship's labourer, who was mentioned by Laurence Mann in his statement. Mr Samuel told the police that he was actually working with Yusef Abdullahi from 3 a.m. onwards, until they left the ship at about 6.30 a.m. Abdullahi seemed perfectly normal to him, not like a man who had just committed a horrific murder. Mr Samuel was not called to give evidence and the Crown Prosecution Service did not pass his statement to the defence until four months after the trial.

Though they could not be as precise as this, other witnesses put Yusef Abdullahi on the ship that night. James Edmond, a welder and fabricator on the *Coral Sea*, told the police, 'I remember sometime on Sunday morning I again came on deck and spoke to the half-caste lad Dullah. I can't remember what we spoke about then. I did not notice anything different about Dullah on the Sunday than when I had seen him on the Saturday.' This evidence was not called.

Only Ronald Williams reported having seen Abdullahi in Cardiff but, in the end, could not be absolutely sure that it was on the night of the murder. Combined with the less well-supported alibis of Stephen Miller and Tony Paris, it seemed the men were well-placed to answer the murder charge.

4

The case against the five accused, so far as there was one, seemed to depend on Stephen Miller being Lynette White's pimp. When she went missing at the beginning of February 1988, it was argued, Miller lost the means of paying for his £60 a day drink and cocaine habit. Lynette White was, in fact, doing business alone from the flat at 7 James Street, which belonged to Leanne Vilday. Vilday had lent, or let, the flat to Lynette and was with Angela Psaila in another flat, two hundred feet away on the far side of James Street. It was alleged – or presumed – that Stephen Miller, in conversation with Vilday on the night of the murder, became aware of the flat at 7 James Street and the possibility that Lynette was there. The case against him was that he owed money to the other men and Lynette White represented the only source of cash. With four companions, he set out on 14 February at about 1.30 a.m., to teach her a lesson. What that lesson was to be, no one knew.

The police later suggested that Miller intended to slap her about, that when this happened there was general excitement. The men had been taking drugs, perhaps enough for them not to remember afterwards where they were or what had happened. During the slapping, someone produced a knife and the lesson was extended to cutting her a few times. In a drug-induced frenzy, this got out of hand and Lynette White's throat was cut.

The prosecution view of what had happened was put to Stephen Miller in a police interview. 'Let me show you all the way through,' the police officer said, describing to Miller what his interiewers believed had taken place. 'Leanne [Vilday] said, "I don't even live here. That's my flat over there." And all of a sudden you know where her flat is. You know where Lynette might be. Yes? You're angry, because it's been building up through the week. You're with mates. They're geeing you up. Something gone on from there, then? Into the flat. There she is. Might give her some slaps a few times. Oop – a knife! Good idea to cut her. And then it goes wrong. It goes very, very wrong.'

But still the evidence for this depended on three witnesses who, if they now told the truth, had been lying in numerous statements for nine months past. Why should they now choose the truth? Leanne Vilday said that it was because her conscience troubled her and she could not sleep at night. If so, it was curious that after her conscience had troubled her she had named three other men as well as the five accused on 6 December 1988 but omitted those three from her further account on 11 December. A good many of her statements to the police could not possibly be true. Were any of them to be believed? Michael Mansfield QC was to describe her bluntly as 'a witness who had lied through her teeth on at least sixteen occasions before Miller was arrested'.

Away from this dangerous territory of witness statements, the forensic evidence, so far as it showed anything at all, indicated that none of the accused men had ever been at the scene of the murder. Not a fingerprint, not a hair, not a bloodstain belonged to any of the five men who were to be tried for the murder, nor was there blood from the witnesses who claimed to have been in the room. To have committed a crime of such violence, causing injury to at least one hand that held the knife, without leaving a trace of evidence must have required cool and deliberate planning. Would the accused men truly have been so meticulous if, as the prosecution suggested, they committed murder under the influence of drink and drugs?

The case, so far as it was based on forensic evidence against the men, was what John Stalker, former Deputy Chief Constable of Manchester, later described as 'a non-starter'. As for the witnesses, he added that he would have been reluctant to bring a car-parking case on the word of such people, let alone a murder charge. But murder had been committed and the blood groupings as well as the palm print on the wall testified that someone other than these men – or perhaps as well as these men – had been present when Lynette White died. It was later suggested that there was more scientific evidence to incriminate the principal prosecution witnesses than there was against the five suspects accused of the murder.

In the investigation of such a crime there was one factor that might still outweigh forensic evidence and alibi witnesses. An admission of guilt, even by one of the accused men alone, could yet lead to the solution of the murder mystery. At the police headquarters building in Cathays Park, South Wales police interviewed the men they had arrested. They did so without much effect, except in the case of Stephen Miller. According to Michael Mansfield, 'One way out was to persuade Miller that he was in the room. Their sole basis was a witness, Leanne Vilday, who shifted her story every time the police interviewed her.' Like his co-accused, Miller had a solicitor present throughout the questioning. It seems, however, that they had not met before and that no one had informed the solicitor of Miller's near-subnormal IQ and his mental age of eleven.

The interviews were tape-recorded, as required under the Police and Criminal Evidence Act 1984. They lasted for fourteen hours, spread over four days. Stephen Miller denied over a hundred times that he had anything to do with the murder or that he had been in the room at 7 James Street when it happened. Despite his IQ and his mental age, he still showed a vigorous defence on the seventh tape, as the questioning got tougher. During the questioning on that tape, the police officer interviewing him left Miller in no doubt of what was to come.

'What we're telling you is fact now. As I told you yesterday, this inquiry has been going for nine or ten months. You were last probably seen some seven months ago – I don't know how many months ago. Since that, we have worked and worked and worked at this to try and solve this absolute malicious, terrible murder, which you say you know absolutely nothing at all about.' – 'I don't.'

'How you can sit there and say that, being in that room, seeing that girl there in the state she was in, and you're supposed to have had all this wonderful care for her. Seeing her damn head hang off and her arms cut and stabbed to death – and you sit there and tell us you know nothing at all about it. Nothing at all about it.' — 'I wasn't there.' — 'How you can ever'…' — 'I wasn't there.' — 'I just don't know how you can sit there, I really don't.' — 'I was not there.' — 'Seeing that girl, your girlfriend, in that room that night like she was. I just don't know how you can sit there and say it.' — 'I wasn't there.' — 'You were there that night!' — 'I was not there.' — 'Together with all the others you were there that night.' — 'I was not there.' — 'And you sit there and say that.'

'They can lock me up for fifty billion years. I said I was not there.' — 'Because you don't want to be there.' — 'I was not there.' — 'You don't want to be there.' — 'I was not there.' 'As soon as you say that you're there, you know you're involved.' — 'I was not there.' — 'You know you were involved in it.' — 'I was not involved and I wasn't there.' — 'Yes, you were there.' — 'I was not there.' — 'You were there. That's why Leanne has come up now ...' — 'No. I was not there.' — ... because her conscience is ...' — 'No.' — ' ... can't sleep at night ...' — 'No. I was not there.' ' ... to say that you were there that night ...' — 'I was not there.' — ' ... looking over her body, seeing what she was like ...' — 'I was not there.' ' ... with a head like she had, and you have got the audacity to sit there and say nothing at all about it.' — 'I was not there.' — 'You know damn well you were there.' — 'I was not there.'

Stephen Miller was classified psychologically as being 'highly suggestible'. He was also said to have had a £60 a day drink and cocaine habit. Even though he thought he had not been present at the murder, perhaps he might be persuaded that he could have been there but did not remember because of the cocaine he had taken earlier that night.

'I didn't touch coke.' — 'Go on then. What was you on? What were you on?' — 'I wasn't on ... Do you know what I was on? Do you want to see what I was on? Weed.' — 'Weed?' — 'Weed.' — 'Did you have coke that night?' — 'No I did not.'— 'You didn't have coke?' — 'No.' — 'But you don't know whether you're there?' — 'Right.'

At this point, Miller had taken a step nearer admitting his guilt, but he drew back from it. His interviewer pursued the possibility that the suspect had been present at the murder but was too 'blocked up' to remember.

'Don't know whether you're there now?' — 'Right.' — 'But there's a possibility.' — 'Weed and coke is two different things.'— 'There is a possibility that you were there that night.' — 'I wasn't there.' — 'There is a possibility.' — 'I wasn't there.' — 'Because we're now coming on to the thing about your alibi and all that and you're now ...' — 'I was not there.' — ' ... and you're now telling us that there is a possibility.' — 'No, I wasn't there.' — 'I think you were there, you see. You were there.' — 'Well then, you think. Then you think. You think.'

The suggestion that Miller was 'blocked up' or stupefied by cocaine was a recurring theme of the interrogation. As another of the CID officers interviewing him put it, 'To the best of our knowledge no one's ever seen you in a stupid state on coke. That could be the case, though. You might have been well blocked up or you might have taken a bit too much or something like that.'

This implication that Miller might have been present at the murder but had no memory of it because of the amount of cocaine he had taken was reinforced by the suggestion that other witnesses and the forensic evidence would tie him to the scene of the crime. There might still be a short period of grace in which he could save himself by confessing or co-operating. After that, his chance would be gone.

'What's happened has happened. Statements have been taken, people have been seen, all forensic evidence been collated. And at the end of an investigation like this people are arrested. Yesterday you were one of those persons. All right? It's been a long, long inquiry. But it's thorough. It's very, very thorough. Now, if you can get yourself out of this, do it. If there's something you want to tell us, and I'm sure – I'm convinced – you want to tell us something, tell us and get it sorted. There are five other people in. They're all being interviewed. There are more coming in as well. You're not in this on your own. But you're the only one who're going to do you any good. Do you understand what I'm saying? Nodding your head?'

'Yeah.'

From time to time Miller seemed ready to admit his guilt and then to withdraw from the admission, as much in confusion as by any deliberate decision. In the end, he gave up the fight. His syntax and word order became chaotic, as in, 'I don't what I've been bullshitting for you now.'

'Why did you go with six other people to No 7 James Street that night?' — 'D'you know what? I want to tell you the truth, honest to God. I don't what I've been bullshitting for you now.' — 'Let's hear it.' — 'I didn't go with them now.' — 'What?' — 'I didn't go with them.' — 'Let's have it.' — 'I didn't. I didn't go there. I didn't go there. I know, so far as I'm concerned, right, that this is, I'm looking at my frigging life, right?' — 'You are. You are. You're looking at a life sentence if this goes wrong.' — 'I know. I admit that I was there.' — 'Right.' — 'Right.'

At last, it seemed, Stephen Miller was prepared to tell the police what they wanted to hear. Subsequently he did so. Was it a confession or had he merely come into line with the statements that other witnesses had made? Had he told the truth at last or merely told the police the story that they had already told him? True or false, it was certainly *prima facie* a full admission of guilt.

'At that time I think Leanne came in. She started shouting, she said something to somebody as far as I could recollect. She said a few words to somebody. She went out. And after that all I can tell is Tony [Paris] just went crazy. So I started stabbing. Do you know what I mean?'

On that December evening, after ten months of investigation, the mystery of Lynette White's death had apparently been unravelled. Stephen Miller had got it 'sorted', for what good that would do him.

5

While Stephen Miller confessed at last, Yusef Abdullahi and Tony Paris continued to deny having been present at the murder or having any involvement in it. Only the two prostitutes who claimed to have been in the murder room implicated Paris. One other witness, Paul Gromek, identified Abdullahi as one of the four black men to whom he had opened the door at about 1.30 a.m. Ronald Williams also thought he had seen Abdullahi in a Cardiff pub at the time when he claimed to have been on the *Coral Sea*. But, of course, Mr Williams later thought he might have been mistaken about the date.

Under interrogation, Abdullahi denied more than five hundred times that he had any part in Lynette White's death. His denials led to clashes with the officers interviewing him.

'You hated Lynette White.' — 'Not at all.' — 'You wanted to see her dead.' — 'Not at all.' — 'You had good reason to see her dead.' — 'Not at all.' — 'You more than anybody.' — 'Not at all.' — 'You thought she'd grassed you out, didn't you?' — 'Not at all.' — 'You're a vicious, evil, wicked man.'

— 'Well that's what you're telling me.' — 'I am telling you.'
— 'Well I don't think I am.' — 'I think you are.' — 'I'm an
innocent man being persecuted.' — 'I think you are.' — 'I'm
an innocent man being persecuted.' — 'You're a disgrace to
the human race.'

Despite all this, Abdullahi, like Paris, insisted upon his
innocence. Neither suspect admitted being at 7 James Street,
let alone having any part in the murder. The police case still
depended crucially upon the confession by Stephen Miller
after thirteen hours of interrogation. Once again, did the
stories of Vilday, Psaila, and Gromek confirm the truth, or
had Stephen Miller been brought into line with those stories?
The question itself was soon central to the case. At the trial,
Miller retracted his confession. But then he found himself in
the classic predicament of a man in such a situation. He was
presented to the jury as a proven liar. Either he had lied to
the police when he confessed his part in the murder or he
was now lying to the court when he denied the contents of
that confession.

By the time that the trial opened in the autumn of 1989, the
five accused men had been on remand in Cardiff prison for
nine months. During that time, it was alleged that Tony Paris
had confessed the murder of Lynette White to another
prisoner, already convicted and serving a sentence of
fourteen years for armed robbery. This new witness, Ian
Massie, added quantity to the prosecution evidence but not
quality. His story was uncorroborated. He was yet another
Crown witness with a criminal record and an obvious motive
for trying to please the authorities.

Ian Massie had been with Tony Paris and his co-accused in
Cardiff prison for over six months. 'In that period I had many
conversations with Tony Paris during which he admitted to
me his involvement in the murder of Lynette White, after
admitting stabbing her and the participation in the murder of
Ronnie Actie, John Actie, Yusef Abdullahi and Miller. I
cannot recall everything that was said in exact detail but have
tried to remember all the pertinent parts. I did not know
Lynette White and neither did I know any of the persons
involved in the murder prior to their arrival at Cardiff
prison.'

Such information from a fellow prisoner was not
uncommon. It had formed part of the evidence against James

Hanratty, as it was to do against Alan Charlton in the case of the 'Body in the Carpet'. Nor was it the first time that Ian Massie had provided information of this sort. Though his evidence formed part of the Crown case, it was soon pointed out that he, like Leanne Vilday and Angela Psaila, stood to gain by helping the police.

The trial was moved to Swansea Crown Court, forty miles away from Cardiff and the risk of jurors being influenced by local feeling. As David Elfer, QC for the Crown, described it, the background to the crime was Butetown, 'an upside-down world, a nocturnal world' where some people carried knives as part of their normal clothing. The proceedings lasted for five months and cost somewhat more than two million pounds. On 26 February 1990, not long before the jury was due to be sent out to consider its verdict, the judge, Mr Justice McNeill, was found dead at the judges lodgings from natural causes. There was nothing to be done but to abandon the trial. The defendants looked 'stunned', as well they might, when it was announced that the Lord Chancellor's department had ordered a retrial. It now became the longest and most expensive murder case in British legal history.

The second trial, with Mr Justice Leonard presiding, began at Swansea in October 1990, by which time the five accused men had been in prison on remand for almost two years. This second case lasted for nearly two months. The witnesses repeated their stories, one of the prostitutes describing the five accused as 'the five monkeys you've got sitting in the dock'. By some quirk, the judge had not heard part of the police tapes of Miller's interviews, including the crucial seventh tape. Not having heard the most aggressive questioning which preceded the confession, he ruled that the taped confession itself was admissible in evidence. Without that confession, convictions would have been self-evidently more difficult to obtain.

As for the content of the police interviews, it was afterwards said that the court and the jurors accepted the evidence of the tapes more easily because solicitors for the defendants were present while they were made, as the police themselves soon pointed out. In Miller's case, however, his solicitor was at a disadvantage in not having been informed of his client's mental age nor his near mental subnormality on the IQ scale.

Significantly, nothing had been revealed by the prosecution about the fact that the mysterious Mr X, a white man, had been the subject of a psychological profile commissioned by South Wales police and that this profile had pointed to him as the most likely killer of Lynette White.

On this basis, the case went to the Swansea jury, which considered its verdicts. The two Actie cousins, John and Ronald, were acquitted. Stephen Miller, Tony Paris and Yusef Abdullahi were convicted of the murder of Lynette White and were sentenced to life imprisonment. Mr Justice Leonard commended the South Wales police investigation of the crime which had been 'obviously very thorough'.

The three convicted men began their protests at once, shouting their innocence at the television cameras as they were taken to the prison bus. The Actie cousins supported them, as did their families. Had a system of capital punishment been in place, however, and had the Police and Criminal Evidence Act not required the tape recording of police interviews, there would have been very little between them and the gallows of Cardiff prison. There might have been protests before their executions but with their deaths the principal witnesses for their innocence would have been removed. Their alibis and their own witnesses had been disbelieved. There was no new evidence of a kind that might have persuaded the Home Secretary to grant reprieves.

Instead of being hanged in the last weeks of 1990, the three men went to their life sentences. A month later, three days before Christmas and some two miles from the James Street flat where Lynette White had been murdered, the body of a Cardiff office worker was found near Fairwater leisure centre. Geraldine Palk was twenty-six and had failed to come home from a Christmas party with office friends in central Cardiff. Like Lynette White she had been repeatedly stabbed, eighty-three times in all. On 10 January, an article in the *Observer* pointed out the similarities in the two murders and speculated on the possibility that they were both the work of the same 'Cardiff Ripper'. South Wales police responded the next day, deploring the harm that such theories would do to the investigation of Geraldine Palk's murder. Their spokesman pointed out that three men had been convicted for the murder of Lynette White and that there were 'eye-witnesses' to the killing. 'Cardiff Ripper Theory Slammed', was the

South Wales Echo headline for 11 January 1991.

There was apparently no new evidence, though there were disturbing reports. The Crown Prosecution Service had failed to disclose a number of witness statements to the defence until after the trial. Whether this was by design or ineptitude was never established. Four months after the trial, on 4 March 1991, Bernard de Maid, solicitor for Yusef Abdullahi, received twenty-two previously undisclosed statements. Among them were those of witnesses supporting the alibis of Miller and Paris.

At the committal proceedings, Angela Psaila had been overheard in the lobby of the court building saying to the police officer, 'How many fucking times have I got to tell you? I wasn't there!' When she was asked in court, during the trial, 'What did that mean?' she replied simply, 'I was at the flat when they murdered Lynette White. I was there and Leanne Vilday.'

For her part, Leanne Vilday now wrote in a letter to a friend. 'I lied to the police just so I could have got out of that fucking police station. I was scared to death.' Leanne Vilday was thought to be a police informer and a policeman had paid one of Angela Psaila's prostitution fines. It was hard to believe that either girl had told the truth, even before these items of gossip were raised. However, in the days of capital punishment, the three men convicted of Lynette White's murder would probably have been hanged before such stories disturbed more than the waterfront air of Butetown.

After the convictions of the three men, their solicitors also put the evidence of Leanne Vilday and Angela Psaila to a controlled test. An actress in the room where the murder had been committed was recorded as she screamed with all her professional power. Sound engineers in the room recorded the screams. In the early hours of the morning, with no other sounds in the street, the screams were played back. The engineers waited in the room where Leanne Vilday and Angela Psaila had been at 1.30–1.45 a.m. on 14 February 1988. Nothing could be heard, even though the engineers were listening for the screams as the witnesses, presumably, would not have been.

The screams were amplified. Eventually they were audible, if one were listening for them, but only at the level of 'a muffled squeak'. On the night of the murder, it seems that even the muffled squeak might have been masked by the noise from a club. Whatever the circumstances, could the cries have carried so piercingly as to have had the two girls running down the stairs and across two hundred feet to the house on the far side of James Street?

Why the Swansea jury convicted the three men remains, by law, a secret of the jury room. It could have been, on the worst grounds, the stigma of Butetown petty crime and the colour of the defendants' skin but that never seemed likely. Perhaps their verdict reflected the old truth that the worst defence of all to a charge of murder is an alibi which is challenged in court by other witnesses and is either disproved or put in serious doubt. Most probably, however, a jury would have convicted the defendants because, even dismissing the so-called 'eye-witnesses' to the murder, they heard Stephen Miller on tape, confessing his crime to the police. What they did not hear was the questioning which preceded this and which reduced him to confusion, if not to tears. They heard him say on the later tape that he and the others killed Lynette White. Why should they think otherwise? The fact that he retracted his confession might simply show that he had been untrue on one occasion or the other. He was a liar, it seemed, and his innocence was compromised by it. After that, if Miller's defence was broken, that of his co-accused would surely be swept away with it.

The protests at the outcome of the trial continued. An audio-tape on which the men denounced the miscarriage of justice was smuggled out of prison and broadcast in BBC news programmes from Cardiff. But then in March 1991 came the first indications that the murder convictions might be overturned in the case of the Darvell brothers, the Swansea dropouts who had been sentenced to life imprisonment in 1986 for the murder of Sandra Phillips, the manageress of a sex-shop in the city. In 1992, their convictions were quashed and the two men set free. In the original trial, much had depended on a confession by Wayne Darvell. Like Stephen Miller and, indeed, like Timothy Evans, he was of low IQ. He was a compulsive confessor and some years before the Swansea killing he had tried to confess to the murder of a dentist in Neath, which he could not possibly have committed. Confessing gained him an importance which he never had otherwise. The attraction of being a suspect in the murder case was, apparently, nothing more than the grandeur of riding in a police car and being the centre of attention.

There was, of course, no direct connection between the case of the Darvell brothers and that of the three men sent to prison for the murder of Lynette White, beyond the fact that an apparently solid conviction in the Darvell case, upheld at first by the Court of Criminal Appeal, had been overturned. This gave renewed impetus to the demand for an appeal hearing in the later case. With the release of the Darvells, the focus of the media moved to the men convicted of killing Lynette White, 'The Cardiff 3', as they were now more sonorously called. When the case was heard by the Court of Criminal Appeal in December 1992, the three men had been in prison since their arrest on suspicion of the crime four years before. Two years had been spent on remand and two years serving their sentences. Despite all that had happened and all that had been learned since the trial, the Crown Prosecution Service prepared to fight on to defend the convictions.

There were many possible issues in the appeal, including the withholding of Tape 7 from the trial jury; the delay in making witness statements available to the defence; the questionable conduct of certain prosecution witnesses. In the event, the basis of the appeal was the exclusion of Tape 7 of Stephen Miller's police interviews from evidence at the murder trial. The jury had heard his confession but not the means by which it was obtained. Had they heard the earlier questioning, in the case of a man of limited intelligence and 'highly suggestible' by psychological assessment, they might well not have convicted him. Without Miller's confession, the case against all three men rested on statements made by principal witnesses with criminal convictions. Against that were alibi statements – far more now than at the trial – made by those who were not beholden to the police or the defendants and were, in that sense, independent.

Tape 7 was played to the Lord Chief Justice and two other judges in the Court of Criminal Appeal. The case went no further than the issue of the interview 'Each member of this court is horrified at hearing that tape,' Lord Chief Justice Taylor said. The interviews had been oppressive and the confession obtained by means of them was unreliable. That in itself made Miller's conviction unsafe. But since the case against Paris and Abdullahi depended fundamentally on Miller's admission that all three were at the girl's flat and had murdered her, the unreliability of that admission undermined the case against them all.

On 16 December, the Court of Appeal gave its reasons for allowing the appeals and setting free the three men. 'Although it was perfectly legitimate for police officers to pursue their interrogation of a suspect with a view to eliciting his account or gaining admissions, and they were not required to give up after the first denial or even after a number of denials, it was undoubtedly oppressive within the meaning of section 76(2) of the Police and Criminal Evidence Act 1984 to shout at a suspect what they wanted him to say after he had denied involvement over 300 times.'

After the successful appeal, South Wales police announced that they had no plans for reopening the case. This presumably meant that they still maintained their view as to who had killed Lynette White or that it was not practicable to pursue inquiries in respect of some other suspect because he was, for example, dead by this time or held in a mental hospital.

Such was the outcome of the Lynette White case. Its details suggest that had the suspects been tried in the days of capital punishment, they would have been hanged. The absence of forensic evidence would not have saved them, as the verdicts against them showed. The fact that Crown witnesses were often those with undisputed criminal records would not have helped them any more than it helped Henry Jenkins or James Hanratty. The unavailability of witness statements to the defence until months after the trial would also have done no more for them than it did for Hanratty. Doubts that were raised, the fact that two merchant ships left Cardiff docks in the hours after the murder with no future check on their crews, or the mysterious role of Mr X, would not have saved the three men any more than the questions raised over Peter Alphon had saved Hanratty. Had it not been for the practice of tape recording police interviews since 1984, the questioning of Miller would have been far less vividly presented. Even in the Court of Criminal Appeal, the impact of such evidence would have been much reduced. The belief that the appeal court provided an automatic safety net had already been disproved in the case of the Darvell brothers, whose appeals had been dismissed in the first instance and who would have gone to the gallows many years before their convictions were quashed.

Miller and his co-accused were fortunate in having the support of a campaign mounted by their families and those in Butetown who believed in their innocence, backed by the civil rights group Liberty and, at last, by the media. But the campaign was given immeasurably greater strength by the fact that the three men themselves were still alive and protesting their innocence. When a man was hanged, the focus of a campaign and, indeed, the principal witness was removed from the scene. There were campaigners of great courage, like the family of Derek Bentley, who fought for forty years and two generations to see justice done. But these were noble and rare exceptions. Far more common were men like Robert Hoolhouse, whose family and sympathizers were bewildered and overwhelmed by the few months of unsought notoriety. Courts of law and the legal process were as strange to them as the customs of the remotest tribes. When the hangman had done his work, such people went on quietly with their lives, kept in their place by the frown of authority.